ROBERT GRANT

The Road to Ruins

AUSTIN MACAULEY PUBLISHERS®
LONDON * CAMBRIDGE * NEW YORK * SHARJAH

A CIP catalogue record for this title is available from the British Library.

ISBN 9781035875061 (Paperback)
ISBN 9781035875078 (Hardback)
ISBN 9781035875085 (ePub e-book)

www.austinmacauley.com

First Published 2025
Austin Macauley Publishers Ltd®
1 Canada Square
Canary Wharf
London
E14 5AA

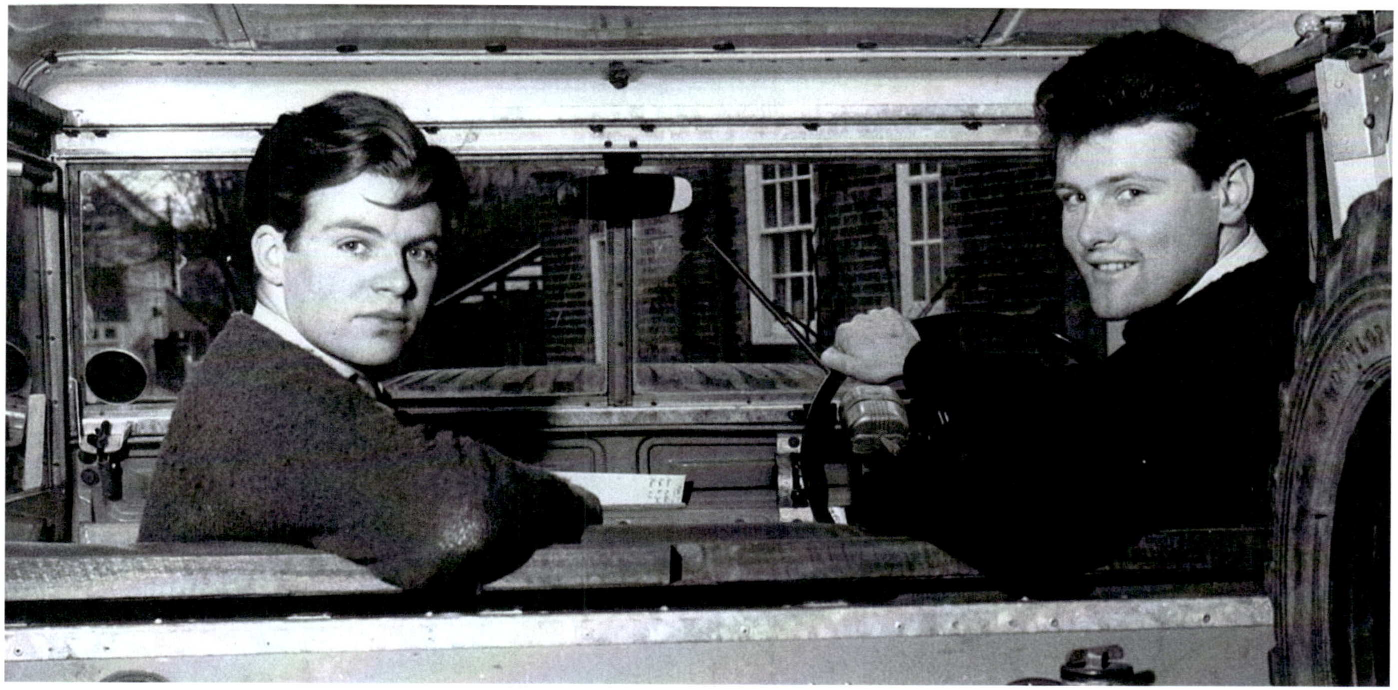

To Gordon, with grateful thanks for spending his hard-earned cash on a life-changing advertisement in *The Times*, October 1963.

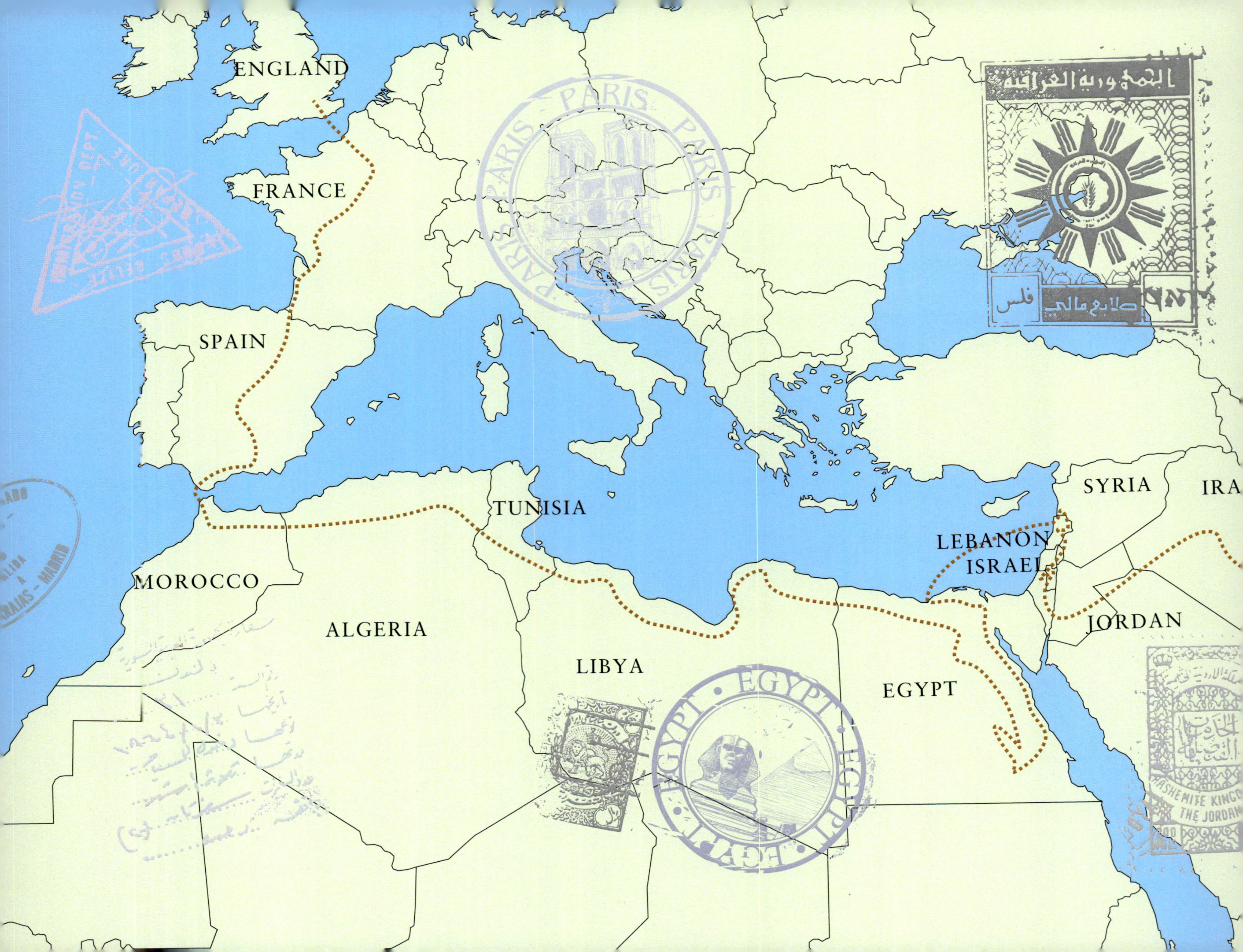
ENGLAND
FRANCE
SPAIN
MOROCCO
ALGERIA
TUNISIA
LIBYA
EGYPT
LEBANON
ISRAEL
SYRIA
IRA
JORDAN
PARIS
EGYPT

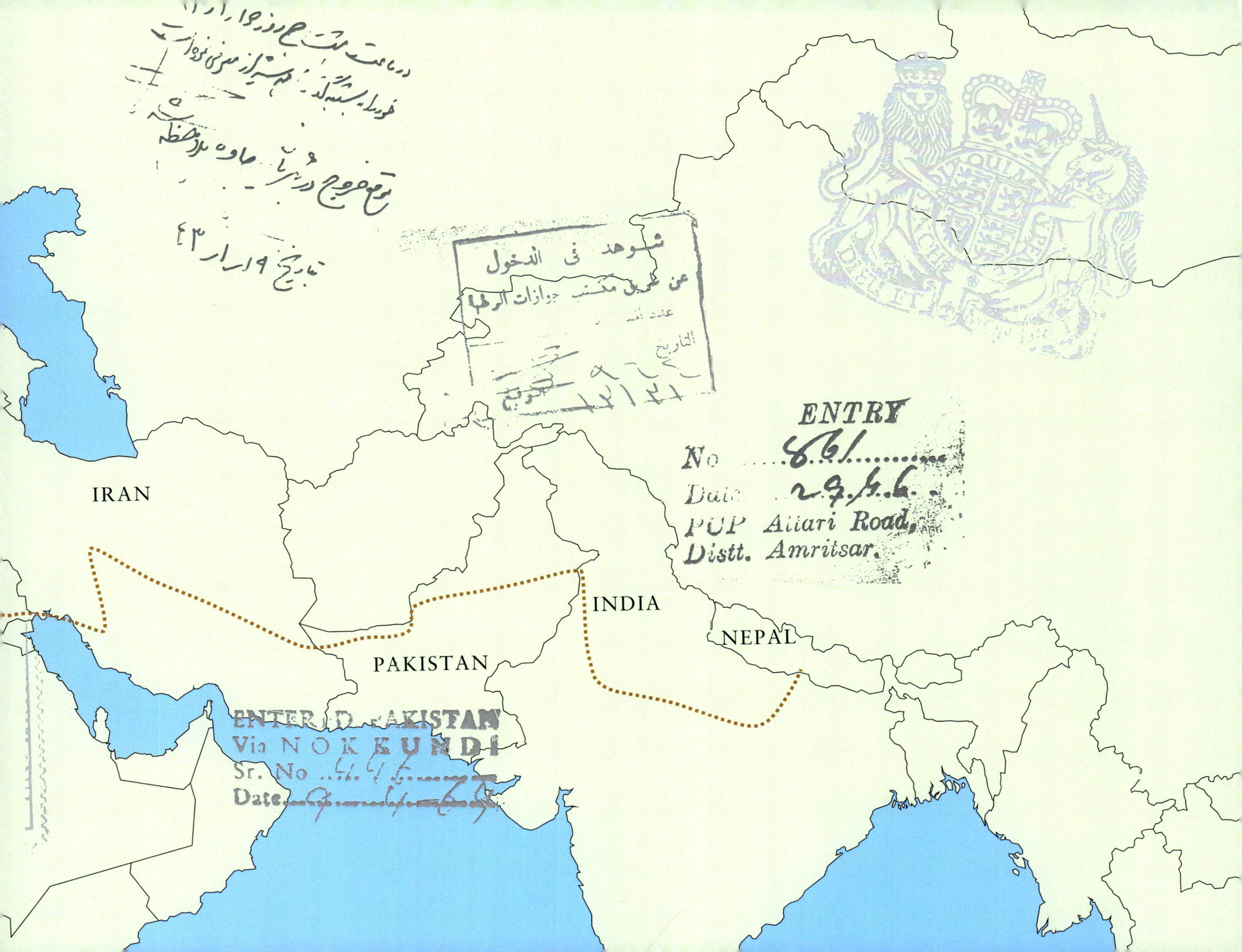

IRAN
PAKISTAN
INDIA
NEPAL
شوهد في الدخول
عن طريق مكتب جوازات الرطبة
ENTRY
No
Date
PUP Attari Road,
Distt. Amritsar.
ENTERED PAKISTAN
Via NOKKUNDI
Sr. No
Date

ACKNOWLEDGEMENTS:

Anthony Barclay Walker, for persistently cajoling me to submit my manuscript to a publisher.

Lyn Marsh, for her encouragement and typing of the manuscript with its many revisions.

Andy Brindle of Clifton Colour Studio, for transposing to disc my 60-year-old photographs.

CONTENTS

Chapter 1

FREEZING EUROPE

London to Gibraltar

IN SOME WAYS, I might owe a debt to the large African gentleman who kicked my knee instead of the ball on the playing fields at the Royal Military Academy, Sandhurst, on that crisp autumn day in October 1962. To literally add insult to injury, I had been ordered to play soccer owing to my previous track record rather than rugby, which I preferred; so, to a degree, maybe destiny played a part.

The injury commanded a typical military response in the form of painkillers, crutches and above all, 'keeping a stiff upper lip'. I must admit that said lip started to quiver somewhat and when on leave a few weeks later my mother noted my leg was the same size as my thigh, which boasted a rainbow-like collection of shades including yellow, purple and red. The swift result of this observation was a visit to a local surgeon, who promptly advised R.M.A. that O/Cdt Grant would not be returning as scheduled as his leg had to be operated on immediately. I was lucky, as the surgeon advised me I had septicaemia and any further delay would have necessitated amputation.

My crutches were returned and replaced with a walking stick and a leg calliper from my thigh to the heel of my George boot. Among other disadvantages it made driving, especially in the bitter, snow-covered months of that winter, extremely tricky. To change gear, one had to lean back and move the leg across to press down on the accelerator. Sudden hard braking was not recommended.

Great consultations followed throughout the remaining winter months, with several visits to the Cambridge Hospital, Aldershot. I did not want to stay in the Army if I was not 100% fit, nor did the Army want to retain me for the same reason. Thus I received an honourable discharge on medical grounds and a pension of £1.2s. per week, although this latter 'benefit' promptly changed as soon as I left the country.

My morale was rock-bottom and my physical state not much better, especially as I had enjoyed supreme fitness, having previously completed the Scots Guards sixteen-week basic training at the Guards Depot, Pirbright prior to qualifying for Sandhurst. Consequently, my mother suggested I go to stay with her oldest friend, who lived in Johannesburg, South Africa. This would give me the opportunity to recover both mentally and physically and to consider my future. After an interminable BOAC Comet flight next to a passenger chain-smoking a cigar, I emerged at Jan Smuts Airport, Johannesburg, feeling akin to a smoked kipper, into bright sunlight and azure skies.

'A whole new world' is an oft-used and maybe laboured phrase but it was certainly the case with me. The vibrancy, the freshness and the spontaneity of the Africans, when not under the cudgel of apartheid, captivated me. I immediately felt an affinity with the continent. When I was a child, my staked-out cycle course in the garden featured an African bend, and I was enthralled with the film *Where no Vultures Fly*, starring Anthony Steel, which was filmed in East Africa and made a huge impact on me. We come to destiny again. My most precious book at prep school was *Wagons Rolling North*, which was an account of the Boers' great trek north from the Cape. My only ever prize at school was an exam of our reading the novel *Prester John*, by John Buchan, about a legendary African chief. Because of this affinity, on my return to England I dictated on my death my ashes be scattered in Africa. That holds to this day.

I couldn't see enough of this effervescent, stimulating and exciting continent. I took a train from Johannesburg to Cape Town and stayed on a fruit farm near Elgin, Cape Town. I visited a sheep and arable farm 100 km into the parched Karoo south of Bloemfontein. I hitch-hiked into the smouldering mountains of Basutoland (now Lesotho), returning with one of their traditional warm and colourful blankets for my mother. I marvelled at the awesome Big Hole in Kimberley, scene of the initial audacious first major diamond 'rush'. Then a diamond sorting house whose ancestral gems formed the foundation of Cecil Rhodes' wealth and empire building. I was totally enthralled by this fascinating country and couldn't have found myself in a better place to recover from the year-long physical and mental strains.

All too soon, my visit was over and I returned to England refreshed, the catharsis of a proposed Army career extinguished but restless and, not least, jobless! However, I couldn't have wished for a more positive recuperation.

Prior to visiting Africa, my great passion was motor sport. From an early age I had followed it closely and could virtually name every car, driver and result from previous decades. This knowledge got me a job as an Editorial Assistant on *Autosport*, the leading UK weekly motor sport magazine, at the time based in dingy offices close to Paddington station in London. My brief was to write race reports, take photographs, edit, research, and source articles. Then, every Tuesday evening with a colleague, paste, cut, cow gum, edit and caption the magazine for publication on the Thursday. This took until approximately 3.00 a.m. at the printers in Stamford Street, London SE1.

I was thoroughly enjoying my 'job', although I didn't regard it as such, as I was in the thick of the just developing, blossoming UK motor sport industry. In addition, I was racing myself ... firstly in an Austin Healey Sprite and then a Lotus 7GT. But, and it was a big but, I was restless. There was a beckoning wide world out there which previously I had known little about. The African itch was itching. I had agreed to join some Oxford graduates who planned to drive overland down Africa to Johannesburg, but this expedition was abandoned owing to a family bereavement. Another such proposal fell through. However, in October 1963, tucked up in the Personal Column of *The Times*, amongst offers for various plush limousines, beautiful mansions and 'genuine pedigree pampered French poodles etc.', I spotted a small, what was to be a life-changing, advertisement headed: 'Young man requires male companion for overland trip to Australia'. I surmised Australia was not quite Africa, but it was in the Southern Hemisphere that I had briefly enjoyed and yearned to see more of. If I didn't make the move now, I would soon be embroiled in another motor racing season, and also there were hints of more responsibility at *Autosport*. I imagined that I could possibly be doing much the same job in thirty years' time! So I wrote to the 'young man', telling him about myself, interests and other relevant facts such as being house-trained and having reasonable mechanical knowledge. Six days later, Gordon Lindsay, having perused his thirty-two replies, phoned, proposing we meet later in the week.

We met at The Bunch of Grapes pub, Old Brompton Road, London, just down from the Brompton Oratory. I arrived in my previously stated tie, tweed jacket and a copy of *Autosport* under my arm. I immediately spotted Gordon (pun intended), which no doubt he will be pleased to hear. He was dressed in jeans, check shirt and old suede shoes, all of which, plus himself, had a liberal spattering of white emulsion.

The pub was crowded with long-haired, pallid-faced young women either talking languidly or animatedly with men who sported hair in equal proportions, wearing tight trousers and pointed shoes. In our corner of the pub, an immaculately dressed gentleman was deep in what appeared a rather surreptitious conversation with an elegant lady who was meekly sipping a gin and tonic.

Gordon lost no time in explaining the situation. He had an uncle who had forsaken his home in Kenya owing to the volatile political situation there and had emigrated to Wagga Wagga (pronounced Wogga!) in New South Wales, Australia. Like myself, Gordon's father had been a pilot killed in the war, and he had no major ties in England. His uncle had sent him glowing reports of the country, friendly people, lovely climate and many opportunities, so he had decided to go and see for himself what it was all about. He proposed to go overland through North Africa, the Middle East, Pakistan and India, then either ship to Perth from Sri Lanka or drive down through Myanmar to Singapore and ship from there. I was lucky he had selected me for the first scrutiny. It was simply an idea at the time; not quite a pipe-dream, but there was a great deal to consider. A suitable vehicle would have to be purchased and equipped, the route planned, visas granted and a thousand and one technicalities and formalities to be completed before departure. As ever, the success of any such venture would be dictated by the planning and preparation: an adage the military has proved fundamental throughout history.

We had a lot in common. Our backgrounds, home life, motor sport interest, Africa – where Gordon had spent his initial childhood – and our lack of enthusiasm for life in what was to us a stifling Britain (even worse today), were very similar. We decided to reflect on our discussions and meet again later in the week, having agreed whether firstly we wanted to embark on such an adventure and secondly to do so together. As a boy I had always wanted 'adventures' and my library was full of R. L. Stevenson, Arthur Ransome, John Buchan, C. S Forester, my worn copy of *The Wonder Book of Daring Deeds* ... and now, potentially, I stood on the threshold of real adventure myself.

I drove home that evening with a whirlwind of thoughts racing through my mind. The air was crisp, and the steady throb of the Mini's engine seemed to engender an atmosphere of purpose and excitement. Did I *really* want to leave England, family and many friends? It meant giving up a lot, not least a career job opportunity which I really enjoyed and a fun and a promising motor sport career. Indeed, the latter was very fraught, but not a consideration at that age. A certain guaranteed way of life to quite the opposite. All these thoughts and many others produced troubled frowns. But what might lie ahead? There was so much to be had, but it wouldn't come to me, so I must go out and get it! Gordon's uncle's phrases of 'great opportunities', 'friendly people', 'fabulous climate' were all endorsing a glimpse of what I had seen in Africa. OK, Australia wasn't Africa, but it was the wide world, south of the Equator, hot and sunny. The British way of life and its climate by comparison I found (and still do) very claustrophobic and uninspiring. I have always been impulsive and very independent and consequently believed there was more to be had in visiting Australia. I believed the Australians' attitude to life was more positive and more liberal-minded. Latterly, I was disabused of this after a few months of living there, where, at that time, the attitude towards the English often verged on the aggressive. Further, their opposition and policies to anyone of colour, particularly the luckless Aborigines, was undoubtedly apartheid in everything but law. If you decide to live in another country, to me it is fundamental you accept their rules and regulations and it is essential to integrate. If you don't, you either 'shut up' or 'get out', but in the case of Australia it was difficult to have an objective discussion. (I had just such a decision to make when in later life I was living in South Africa during the iniquitous regime of apartheid. Objecting would have quickly found me in prison, so I left.)

The Brits, or 'POMS' as the Australians referred to them, came from the aftermath of the era of the ten pounds emigration scheme, when many of the new arrivals constantly complained about conditions and referred to their preferences for 'back home'. Australians not surprisingly responded to these criticisms in no uncertain terms that perhaps said moaner should 'return home', but not quite in those words!

The 'I'm all right Jack' attitude in Britain particularly rankled with me. I believed if one was prepared to get one's head down and work hard, the opportunity was there to be maximised. Too much relied on having been to the 'right' school and consequently knowing the 'right' people. Nowadays it's almost the reverse ,and further factors perhaps are considered such as race, gender origin or religion. Of course, having experienced it in Africa, the climate in every respect was an improvement; the outdoor life was just not wishful thinking, and everything about living in Australia (which on the face of it had no divisive racial policies – again, I was wrong there) appeared healthier and more open. I considered the then Australian perceived fear of what they termed 'The Yellow Peril'. This was their concern at mass immigration, principally from Asia and the Far East. But surely room for many, many more with the then denser population areas hugging the coasts. I concluded that when that did become a problem no doubt such concerns would be worldwide.

By the time I had covered the twenty-five miles back to Chalfont St Giles, I had decided that if Gordon was willing I would drive with him overland to Australia.

We met again at the end of the week and agreed a provisional starting date of 1st February 1964. We knew that detailed preparation would go a long way to the ease and success of the trip. We set about mapping out a plan with agreed responsibilities. The priority, needless to say, was to source a suitable vehicle, and it didn't take much thought to target a proven, sturdy Land Rover. Buying second-hand cars, let alone in the '60s, for such an important journey demanded caution but, as luck would have it, I knew of someone who had such a vehicle for sale. Destiny again?

Within a week, we had test-driven a Land Rover and bought it! The vehicle had already been to Australia and 'knew' some of the route, which we thought would be an advantage! A friend who had lived in Australia for two years had shipped the car from England to Sydney. He then equipped it for long trips into the bush hinterland, which was termed 'bundu bashing'! After his stay there, he decided to ship the Land Rover back to Britain, but when the boat got to Bombay (now Mumbai), he arranged to pay the £60 for the car to be unloaded and then drove back via India, Pakistan, Iran and Europe.

At that time 'the hippy trail', as it was known, traversed Europe to Istanbul and then down through Turkey, Iraq, Iran, Pakistan to India and was a very popular route. Quite where some of these travellers were heading for or finished up was a matter of speculation. Countless VW combis with unshaven 'artistic' characters wreathed in sweet-smelling smoke was a somewhat harsh popular misconception but nonetheless to a degree was based on fact. We surmised that in later life it would be much easier to see Europe rather than the then relative calm of the remote, major archaeological sites of North Africa, Egypt and the Middle East. As world events would prove, we weren't far wrong in that assumption.

This overland trip took Edward 28 days. The Land Rover was long-wheelbase and had only done 30,000 miles, so was in good overall condition. It had numerous valuable extras such as free-wheeling hubs, Kangaroo protective bars (which are a constant hazard of driving in less populated areas of Australia) across the front and an ex-R.A.A.F. compass. Very importantly, it had an extra underfloor 50 gallon fuel tank so, coupled with the standard tank, we had a total capacity of 64 gallons. Needless to say, this was a vital asset given the distances we were to cover, which were not noted for their proliferation of fuel stations. There was also an extra tank for water, but we decided to contain this crucial liquid in two five-gallon plastic jerry cans on the grounds of cleanliness and ease of use.

We drew up long lists of required items under various headings such as Supplies (i.e. provisions), Medical, Mechanical Equipment, Maps/Route (this to include as many major archaeological sites as possible), Formalities/Visas/Carnets, etc. I gave my notice to leave *Autosport* at the end of December 1963, when I was lectured over a farewell lunch by the Advertising Director telling me I was totally mad and throwing away a promising career. My attitude to that (although I didn't respond) was that he was probably a member of the Flat Earth Society.

This left the icy, slippery month of January to get everything sorted and stowed. I wrote to countless firms, a different one to each, telling them of our route, objectives and ultimate goal. Could they kindly please consider donating some of their valuable product in return for testing and endorsement from some pretty unusual places? Most requests were declined on the grounds they didn't supply 'expeditions', but in nearly every case they wished us well. We wrote to the Automobile Association requesting maps of our proposed route. They were able to send a few with a letter telling us they hadn't got many maps of our intended route but in due course could we please advise them of roads, etc., for future reference! One company did us particularly proud, donating four large boxes of loo rolls in delicate shades of white, green, blue, violet and yellow! Since everyone then believed if you consumed anything outside Britain you were bound to get severe stomach problems, we decided to take them but were not quite sure if they wanted references! The two other 'major donations' were a mountain of Brillo pads and a large supply of Macleans toothpaste.

There was no need to enact the old Cerebos advertisement by putting salt on our tails since we were rushing about making the final arrangements both day and night. I was driving to and from London on a daily basis, with my mother stalwartly relaying various messages and phone calls. Our avowed principle was to sort out and source as much as possible any required or anticipated paperwork before departure rather than be held up en route. Insurance for the car, baggage, cameras and medical equipment/expenses was agreed – though quite how we would make a claim from the Sahara or deepest Iran was not considered. The Libyan, Egyptian, Syrian, Lebanese, Iraqi and Iranian Embassies all required huge forms to be completed, together with personal visits. The photofit machine in Baker Street tube station eventually jammed with the strain of having to take thirty photos each of both of us!

We constructed our beds in the back of the Land Rover: two wooden notched cross pieces at each end, which anchored three aluminium tubes – one at each side and one in the middle, then threading through a strong canvas sheet. Quick to erect, dismantle and stow. It also ensured we could lock ourselves into the car whilst sleeping, which was to prove an invaluable precaution. Rover Ltd gave the car a complete 'Safari' overhaul, and Gordon attended their two-day course near Solihull, where he drove on their demanding cross-country test track and received much advice on mechanics, fault identification and repairs for the marque. Again, an invaluable investment. We had one spare wheel carried in the car so fitted another bolted to the bonnet, which was also secured with padlocks. A vice was fitted to the tailboard and a further lock on the fuel cap. After the course at Land Rover, we bought and stowed a recommended range of essential spares.

Each successive week we suffered two days of useless left arms having visited the vaccination centre for an alarming cocktail of injections. This was to have consequences on New Year's Eve, as a combination of typhoid/plague vaccination did not seem to mix well with appropriately celebratory liquids! Various leaving parties took place, with lightning farewell visits to friends and relations – one of whom, after telling me I was completely mad, insisted we should be well armed 'as the fuzzy-wuzzies can be very unpredictable'! We ignored such recommendation on the basis that if we were in a tight spot and produced a weapon it would probably exacerbate an already volatile situation. By the final week of January, all our supplies had come through and my bedroom looked like an embarkation point for the D-Day landings. Besides our expedition supplies, we had to consider any required baggage for life at our eventual destination.

In addition to our 72 packets of soap pads, we added six dozen boxes of matches and two boxes of lifeboat flamers (just as good in a sea of sand) courtesy of Bryant and May. For personal hygiene, we had cartons of toothpaste and enough loo rolls to stretch from Tangier to Cairo. John Bell & Croyden of Wigmore Street kindly discounted medical supplies, not least penicillin and Sulphamezathine (hopefully a 'cure-all'), derived and used by the Romans and the Sioux! Knorr did us proud with foil sealed packets of soup and lemonade powders, which were not only nutritious but easy to pack. Two large, discounted rucksacks were to contain our clothing and any personal kit. Also sand fly nets, two sleeping bags, blankets and a towel each. For cooking, we included two small gas canister cookers, a frying pan, saucepan, tin opener (vital!), two tin mugs, plates, knives and forks, as we didn't anticipate any dinner parties. That most essential liquid, namely water, would be carried in the two five-gallon plastic containers. These would be decanted into our own hand-plunger plastic filter bottles. Throughout, our thinking was to take only essentials to save both weight and space. Although we were both non-smokers, except to discourage mosquitoes, Rothmans of Pall Mall generously donated an initial thousand cigarettes with a further thousand to be collected in Gibraltar. These proved to be the best possible forms of payment or response to 'baksheesh' demands. The final item was a large plastic container which when filled with water and some kindly donated 'Tide' washing powder would be converted by the car's progress and subsequent vibrations to our own 'washing machine'. It worked!

This all had to be stowed flat behind the two front seats so we could erect our canvas bed on top of them. We also had a hidden padlocked locker under the passenger seat to secrete (or so we thought) vital paperwork, cameras, passports, etc.

On the 4th February 1964, I drove up the drive from home to London. My mother told me she wondered if she would ever see me again – she did, seven years later – and never forgot the tail lights disappearing down the road. My Labrador, Sam, kept on looking for me for months. I spent the night on a friend's sofa in his flat in Queensgate and then collected Gordon from a similar situation in Gunther Road, Earls Court. More passport-type photos were extracted from the nearby tube station, and then it was pedal to the metal for the cross-channel ferry from Dover. Our dawn start was to prove futile, as when we called in at the AA office we discovered the promised insurance documents hadn't arrived. In spite of cajoling the local Post Office, hoping to source this vital piece of paper, we missed our 11.00 a.m. cross-channel booking to France. Nothing for it but to 'do' Dover instead of 'doing' Boulogne, admittedly most of it from the back row of the 3/9d in the local cinema.

At last we collected our insurance confirmation and boarded a ferry to Dunkirk further up the French coast. We had a very rough crossing but Gordon assured me that 'as long as the peas didn't roll off the plates' we would be OK. And so it proved, albeit arriving in France half an hour late at 11.00 p.m. After a few slippery excursions on the icy roads of France we made our first halt near St. Omer. I remember looking back from the ferry at the iconic white cliffs of England and wondering what was before us and if I would ever see them again. Quite a momentous 24 hours.

However, after all the frenzied preparations and once the porridge container had been removed from under Gordon's rear, we were soon asleep. We overslept on our first morning in France as the Land Rover had taken on the role of a mobile deep freezer. Waking up wasn't helped by the fact our eyelids were frozen together and to wash and shave in the sub-zero temperature wasn't that attractive! Such was the icy weather that we decided to press on and prepare breakfast when we and the ingredients had thawed out. As it happened the food, in spite of being cooked, was quickly as cold as the cooks.

We stopped at Evreux for a hot coffee and then on to Chartres – site of one of the three major examples of Gothic French architecture, the others being at Rheims and Amiens. The cathedral was reconstructed on the foundations of an earlier church which had been destroyed by fire and was consecrated in 1260. It is particularly famous for its 176 stained glass windows, with the glass donated by the local guilds between 1210 and 1240. During both World Wars the windows were dismantled piece by piece and stowed for safety.

As ever with these vast Catholic-built edifices, the cathedral dominated the skyline and the bustling town of Chartres nestled below. The interior was warm spiritually but otherwise there was no escape from the bitter cold.

Chartres cathedral, west side

Above: One of 176 stained glass windows
Opposite: Chartres Cathedral

Chartres cathedral, south side

We pressed on to Tours on the confluence of the Loire and Cher rivers for a rapid baked bean dinner. Then after covering a further 80 miles, giving us a total of 370 for the day, the mobile freezer was stopped for the night beside a memorial to Marcel Renault, who was killed in the 1370-km motor race from Paris to Madrid in May 1903. Two hundred and twenty-four cars started this event, but Renault was delayed by huge crowds and dust. On reaching Poitiers he had progressed from 60th position to be amongst the leaders, but he tragically crashed shortly afterwards. Such was the toll

of deaths and accidents to both drivers and spectators the French authorities halted the race at Bordeaux. Subsequently the competing cars had to be independently transported to Vitoria, Spain, to continue to the finish. Marcel Renault's memorial was destroyed by the Germans in WW2 but restored after hostilities. A nice coincidence that two motor sport adventurers should stop at this site!

Marcel Renault memorial, Poitiers

After another bitterly cold night, we woke up to a large film of ice covering the inside of the Land Rover as well as the outside. We scraped off enough to get going, but even with the aid of a watery sun it stayed until midday. Such sun encouraged to us forge south as fast as possible through the famed wine region around Bordeaux, then across the flat, featureless plain of Les Landes: nothing but sandy scrub and pine trees, which reminded me of the gorse-covered military landscapes of Aldershot and Salisbury Plain. Our first tyre decided to give up just 15 miles short of Bayonne, but a cheery French lorry driver kindly lent us his jack to change the wheel, which was much quicker than ours! We were already reduced to one spare wheel and not even out of France so were not impressed to discover the tyre had not been replaced. We caught a glimpse of the chilly, intimidating Atlantic at Biarritz and the brooding, snow-covered Pyrenees looming ahead.

No hold up at Customs and into the Spanish foothills. We had made good progress, spurred on by the thought of warmer climes further south, and had already covered 680 miles in France and 158 in Spain. We added another 120 miles and reached the highest point of the journey in Europe at Burgos, 2805 feet above sea level. The latter part of the drive before a halt was almost continuously uphill, with our passing more lorries than cars.

Foothills of the Pyrenees

We were getting used to the igloo-like, iced conditions on waking up, but at least this morning we didn't have to push start or roll downhill and drop the clutch to encourage a frozen engine into action. After only 20 miles, we noticed that the water temperature was registering 100 degrees, which is not recommended. We removed the radiator cap and waited for the heat to dissipate, at the same time contemplating the unwelcome possibility of changing a warped cylinder head. Luckily, the problem was lack of water, which we hadn't spotted in the dark as the dashboard lights weren't on. It was fortunate we had seen this before the engine overheated!

Above and below, bridges over Tagus towards town.

River Tagus

We pressed on across a high plateau flanked by snow-covered mountains towards Madrid. The locals too were feeling the cold, trudging along beside a loaded donkey or a horse and cart with their hands in their pockets and blankets over their heads. We found the official Land Rover agent in Madrid, who supplied us with a new Firestone tyre at half the price for the one we had bought in England, even with a 25% discount!

After Madrid, we followed the recommended AA route to enjoy the compact historical town of Toledo. We encountered myriad uninviting, non-Land Rover-accommodating, narrow streets but eventually found parking and the opportunity to explore on foot. Toledo was known as the 'Imperial City', as it was the main venue for the court of Charles V. After the fall of the Roman Empire, it became the capital of the Visigoth's Kingdom of Hispania. From as early as 500 BC it became famous for its production of steel weaponry, not least swords and scabbards. As ever, it is dominated by a massive cathedral and the Fortress of Alcazar.

Town of Toledo

Main entrance to walled town of Toledo

Primatial cathedral of Saint Mary of Toledo

Toledo cloisters

Misty view over the town of Toledo

Left: Southern tower of the cathedral. Right: Typical Toledo street.

Outer town walls of Toledo.

After our visit to Toledo, we continued for another 60 miles and were glad to enjoy somewhat milder temperatures and consequently a less hasty dinner. We were settling into a routine of early starts, a hot breakfast and then pushing on to the evening's halt, with no 'site-seeing', as all the while we were anxious to have the icy conditions behind us and enjoy some sun. Instead of cutting across Spain direct to Malaga and the coast, we continued due south to Granada and the Alhambra Palace. 'Alhambra', translated, is 'the red', reflecting the colour of the red clay which surrounds the fort. It was originally built as a fort in AD 99, mainly by Christian slaves, who 'lived' in nearby subterranean caves. Then, in the mid-13th century, it was restored and extended to the present palace by Yusef I, Sultan of Granada. We approached, skirting the edge of the hill which gave way to the Palace perched above the bustling city of Granada. The view from the battlements over the city was spectacular. Before we could access the Palace, we had to calm a very excited attendant who demanded 100 pesetas for parking in the street on a Sunday and a horde of local ladies demanding money for reasons we had no way of understanding.

Most of the morning was spent in the main enjoying, without the usual throng of tourists, the buildings and gardens of the complex, all dominated by the surrounding snow-capped Sierra Nevada mountains. After a late lunch of fried salami, eggs, bread and marmalade with coffee, we headed west parallel with the southern coast of Spain. This route took us through a very hilly region, with endless low-gear hairpin bends and climbs.

Alhambra Palace, Granada

Palace gardens with Keep

Palace gardens

View from Palace of Granada

Moorish architecture, including courtyard, fountain and ornamental pool

We reached the matching blues of the sea with the sky at Malaga and then pressed on another 80 miles to Gibraltar. We had made swift progress from Dunkirk but, not least given our lack of winter clothing, were anxious to reach some warmer climes. Our time in Spain was brief, but we had enjoyed our visit, particularly the magnificence of the Alhambra. It was obvious that life was hard here, but the locals were friendly and helpful, especially given neither of us could speak a word of Spanish. We had intended to find a room locally and enjoy the luxury of a bath, but since the cheapest rooms were 7/6d we decided to stay in the Land Rover. We met up with a friend of Gordon's who entertained us with a few beers at 'The Rock', which was Gibraltar's most prestigious hotel at the time.

Gibraltar

Local residents

Gibraltar runway with Algeciras beyond. Note: gun emplacements in foreground.

Chapter 2

BACK IN AFRICA

Morocco, Algeria and Tunisia

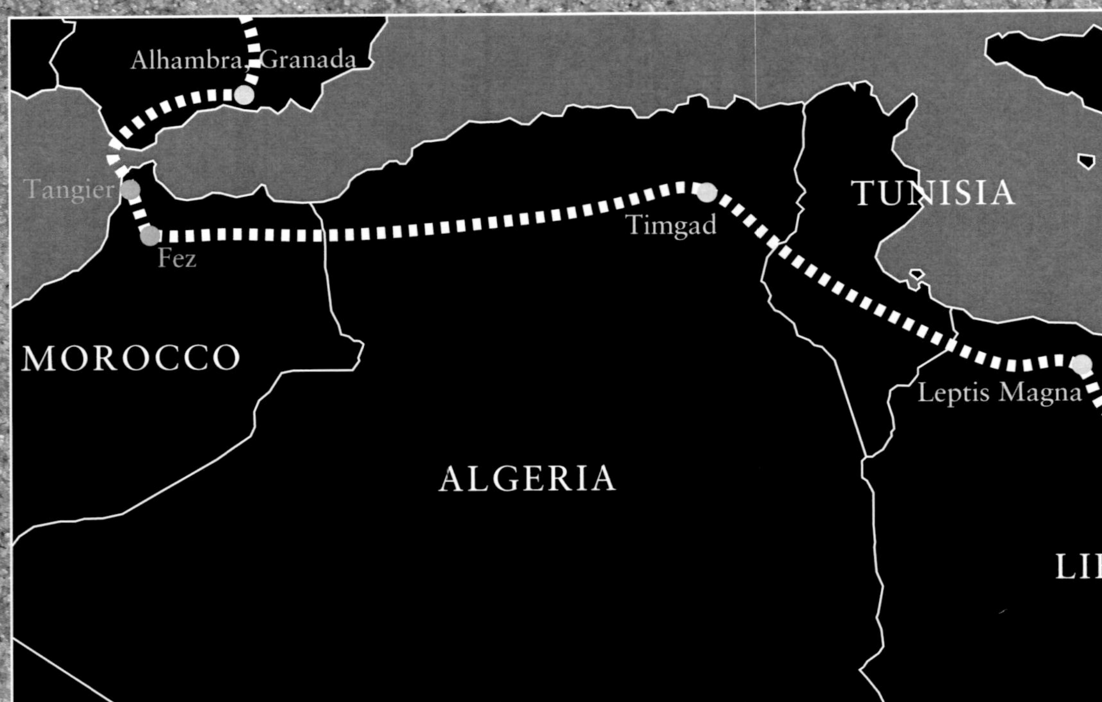

JIMMY, GORDON'S FRIEND, generously let us enjoy a bath at his home the following morning, which was a real treat, and then we were off to explore England again… or very nearly. Everywhere and everyone appeared British, including policemen in identical uniforms, symbolic bright red telephones and post boxes. The only non-British were the daily influx of Spaniards who arrived there to work. It was a pleasant change not having to rush off in the car, and we were able to take our time 'site-seeing'.

The much-welcome sun was high, and soon we were up on the Rock itself, where we met the many resident apes. We admired the ingenious water collection reservoirs built at the bottom of the eastern face of the Rock so they could collect the rainwater flowing down from the steep, concreted slopes of the mountainside. More history with the gun emplacements and St Michael's Cave, named after a similar grotto in Italy where the Archangel Michael is said to have appeared. The ever-hospitable Jimmy took us out to a magnificent lunch, and it was quite an effort to return to our lay-by-parked Land Rover and set about some serious servicing. That afternoon, we completely unloaded the car and moved stores, water cans, etc., to more strategic positions. We discovered Rover Ltd hadn't changed the oil seals and a universal joint covering had to be replaced, which luckily we heard fall off somewhere in France! An exhaust gasket had blown, and most of the sump nuts were loose. Although we were both non-smokers we duly collected the 1000 cigarettes that Rothmans had kindly donated and decided they would be ideal 'baksheesh/bargaining' currency. We bought another jack, replaced the spare wheel and checked oil, fuel and water ready for our early ferry departure from Algeciras to Tangier in the morning, which was a short drive down the coast.

Tangier harbour

Tangier

View of the City

The Casbah (market)

Left: Snake charmer welcome. Right: Tangier street scene

Kairaouine mosque, the largest in N. Africa

2.5 km perimeter wall around the mosque

Town of Fez

'Crash' on arrival in Tangier at 11.00 a.m. after a two-hour crossing, we were suddenly in a totally new world, AND I was back in Africa! I experienced a combined sense of elation, accomplishment of ambitions to a degree achieved and a somewhat nervous anticipation of what lay before us. The foreseen inquisition of two young itinerant Europeans by the Customs did not materialise, and the first greeting we encountered was from an Arab snake charmer. After a very close encounter with an adder in my childhood I have a phobia of snakes, so Gordon kindly did the honours. We decided to park the car near the Casbah, which is the Arab quarter of Tangier and from there proceeded on foot. Whilst two gentlemen were fighting as to whom would be our guide, we were being given a detailed itinerary by an opportunist colleague! The jail, the Royal Palace, a carpet-making house and the market were all part of the tour, but throughout we were appalled by the obvious poverty and squalor, which must be even worse in the heat of the summer months. Just over a week previously, we had been sublimely enjoying the ambience and comforts of South Kensington, and this was quite a contrast!

Leaving Tangier, we drove parallel to the Mediterranean Sea for the first few miles and then headed south to cover the 200 miles to Fez, where we halted for the night. I knew I was back in Africa as soon as I saw the golden sunset, which, prejudicially, I consider unique to that continent! We had been advised not to drive in North Africa after dark, so we embarked on a new routine of turning in at dusk and rising at dawn.

Street scene Fez

Fez is the Mecca of the Western Islamic world and one of the four Imperial cities of Morocco, the others being Marrakesh, Meknes and Rabat, the capital. It possesses many beautiful mosques, not least the Kairaouine Mosque, which dates from the ninth century and is still Morocco's largest religious building. It is also considered the world's oldest university, having been founded in 859. The city was founded by Idris Ben Abdallah, who was a descendant of the prophet Mohammed. It quickly grew in population, swelled by the expulsion of many Arab families from Spain. Fez is almost an oasis in the surrounding scrub and sandy countryside. Whilst wandering around the grounds of the Imperial Palace, we met a young Frenchman who elected to be our guide in exchange for 80 Rothmans cigarettes. We started at the Medina, which was like a latent time-warp and much larger than the Casbah in Tangier; another world completely, with a confusing myriad of claustrophobic streets housing a host of competing, crowded, noisy shops and shopkeepers. We saw many mosques but, not being Muslims, we were forbidden to enter. We met a storekeeper who had certificates assuring that his metal goods were the best in Morocco. There seemed to be a street for each different trade, which included apothecaries, milling, metalwork, carpentry and wool dying. We visited the world-famous Chouara tanneries, where the tanners were kneading hides, standing waist-deep in vast vats containing different colours of dye. The smell was appalling, emanating from a toxic mix of chemicals, but the end product was unique. Carpet-making was another traditional trade, but in spite of mint tea-flavoured invitations, we were unable to consider any negotiations. Tempting but impractical, as there was no spare room in the Land Rover for souvenirs, nor could our tight budget allow for such purchases. We were well and truly in the wider world, which we knew was out there but had absolutely no idea of the contrasts to our own hitherto comfortable, sheltered existence.

Arms and metal workshop

Tanneries

We left Fez in a howling wind and pushed on across a 100-mile, flat, featureless plain with the snow-capped Atlas Mountains in the distance. After 410 miles and a total equivalent of 26 shillings spent in Morocco, we crossed the frontier into Algeria, and after climbing to some 2000 feet, we encamped at Tlemcen.

Founded in 1236, the Kingdom of Tlemcen became part of the Ottoman Empire in 1554. It was a key hub of the ancient trading route from Oran right across the Sahara to Western Sudan.

Next morning, we set out early and had ambitions of achieving a hefty mileage, but it was not to be. Shortly after Oran, we stopped on the road at Montugen for lunch and a Mediterranean swim, but the sun refused to co-operate, so we set about trying to cash a traveller's cheque. We were hungry, and the Land Rover was thirsty, but our request proved too demanding (literally!) for the bank tellers. Thus, we managed another 80 miles to Orleansville, where it was imperative we sourced some local currency. This process took nearly two hours, but luck was with us, as we met a Frenchman who introduced us to an American who kindly cashed an American Express note. Now, with both personnel and vehicle replete, we covered another 366 miles and arrived well after dark on the outskirts of Algiers. We considered ourselves very lucky, as we chose a nice palm tree-lined area overlooking the light-twinkling city.

Approaching the Sahara desert

Oasis, northern Sahara

The following morning, as I climbed down from the car, I noticed an armed sentry watching me closely. We later discovered that 'the quiet road' we had chosen was where all the French military and Government officials lived, and our parking place was right in the grounds of their military GHQ: an immediate and obvious target for any trouble from the recently occupied locals!

For decades, Algeria had been part of France's empire and was divided into three French 'Departments': Oran, Constantine and Alger. Some 80 years earlier, fermentations of independence grew with the formation of FLN (Front Liberation Nationale), and terrorist violence became commonplace. In spite of visits and promises from many French Government ministers, not least President Charles de Gaulle, Algeria ultimately achieved independence two years previous to our arrival. This explained the pervading presence of a token force of French military and administrative officials. We were promptly 'detained' and taken to the Commanding Officer, who questioned us extensively before we were released and escorted off the encampment. No doubt the lax sentries of the previous evening had an equally uncomfortable interview with him!

We decided it was best to take breakfast elsewhere, in spite of the dramatic view afforded by our overnight venue – sometimes compared with that of the French Riviera, ironically enough. We asked umpteen policemen for the street which housed Barclays Bank to no avail, but at least we were getting to know the city of Algiers quite well. Stopping at a local café for stimulating coffees caused much curiosity from the locals and probably overt suspicion, given the recent political upheavals. When we eventually did find the bank, it was closed – after all, it was Valentine's Day, no doubt of more importance to the French! We managed to cash a cheque at an hotel and then muddled our way out of the city.

In many ways, we had the advantage of ignorance and naivety about the local, somewhat volatile, atmosphere and blissfully journeyed avoiding political discussion and its ramifications. In so many encounters with local people we were judged and responded to at literally face value.

Soon we were up in the hills, attaining a level of 3,500 ft before crossing a magnificent pass in the Massif de l'Ouarsenis mountains, which was above the snowline. Instead of pressing on down the one main central road east, we diverted to Bou-Saada on the edge of the Sahara. We reached there in the early afternoon but soon concluded that the promotional pamphlet had rather excelled itself, as it was seemingly more like a busy town than the promised oasis, so we decided to press on another 120 miles to Biskra. The terrain was similar to the previous stretch, without the undulating, sand-shifting dunes of popular conception. However, it soon became more interesting, as we passed through several real oases with palm-fringed encampments. Suddenly, part of the road was blocked by a huge sand drift, but luckily, with four-wheel drive, we were able to get around it.

Timgad

Eventually, we reached Biskra and parked up in a quiet spot amongst all the Arab houses. In front of us was a classic 'Beau Geste' fort with a tower at each corner, crenellated walls and a huge, heavy-barred, studded central double door. I was sitting in the driver's seat writing up my diary when suddenly I felt this cold pressure on the side of my neck. I glanced down and noted it was a rifle pressing against me.

'You are spies,' said the trigger-gripping owner, 'taking notes of our fortifications.'

'I know I was at Sandhurst,' I replied, 'but this is ridiculous.'

The man with the rifle and his several colleagues took quite a bit of persuading that we were just two tourists. After I showed them my diary they eventually believed us and encouraged, indeed insisted, we leave immediately, which we did, to spend the night at the edge of the village.

Ironically, although we were as close to the real Sahara desert as we would ever be, it rained incessantly all night. It eased up somewhat the next day and then added a hail storm for variety.

We set off at dawn and had our first sight of nomadic Arabs. They carried everything with them, including their skin tents, and were herding a mix of camels, donkeys and sheep. Obviously, some to work and some to eat.

During the morning, we visited the astonishingly well-preserved Roman city of Timgad (meaning 'peak' or 'summit') in the Aures mountains. It was founded by the Emperor Trajan in AD 100 as a military colony and was primarily populated (approx: 15,000) by Roman veterans who were there as a buffer against marauding Berber tribes. It was surrounded by over a thousand acres of farmland, rendering it almost self-sufficient.

It is one of the best-preserved examples of a grid plan as used by Roman town planners. A major contributing factor to its preservation was due to it being covered by sand in the 7th century. The 12-metre-high sandstone Arch of Trajan is a major dominating feature. The 3,500-seat theatre, with its extraordinary acoustics, still sometimes hosts productions. In addition, we inspected the first basilica and forum, all of which were in an amazing state of preservation.

'A mess of porridge' masqueraded as lunch, and at the next town of Ain Bidal we converted all our remaining Algerian currency into petrol, which we calculated would see us through Tunisia. We crossed the border in the early afternoon, leaving behind the 'Votez Oui' and 'Vive Ben Bella' signs, which were part of the Algerians' struggle for independence from France. There was long-standing resentment of France's colonisation (nothing new there in relation to Africa) of the country after they arrived in 1851. The French then proceeded to implement their policy of '*razzia*', which basically was a free-for-all rampage of destruction and looting. This was followed by mass immigration from France, and the majority of the revenues these settlers generated was remitted to the mother country with subsequent little benefit to the locals. Ahmed Ben Bella had been highly decorated while serving in the French army and subsequently became one of the founder principals of the National Liberation Front.

Trajan's Arch

Looking north from Trajan's Arch

Reverse view from Trajan's Arch

Museum

Theatre

Floor mosaics

General view from the theatre

Gordon, main road

We completed 416 miles, with the latter part seemingly interminable with scarcely a bend in the road. We had intended to visit two further sites of ruins, but with no detailed maps or local communication we were unable to find them. Sadly, the only ruins we saw were either on two legs or four wheels!

We were getting into our new routine of very early 'bed' and similarly early starts, which were often boosted by an egg breakfast. However, the local chicken eggs are much smaller than we were used to, thus twelve local eggs would probably be the equivalent of three English ones.

After passing through Medenine, which is one of the largest troglodyte villages in North Africa, we reached the Tunisian border. The process of passing through the formalities of passports and carnet examination seemed endless, with no less than four different checkpoints. We met two Italians whose car had broken down and gave them a lift to Tripoli. That stretch was the usual flat, uninspiring, hazy horizon motoring with high winds constantly blowing drifting sand across the road. Tripoli found us on the usual money search, and after having been refused by the best-looking hotel in Tunis to change our travellers' cheques, we made a fruitless tour of the city. So, drawing a blank, we returned to the hotel. With a different reception clerk, no problem – we were in funds again! Lunch was partaken at Rose's Tea Garden, no less, and then we pressed on for the evening's halt, taking care not to be near any military houses after our Biskra and Algiers experiences.

Troglodyte village

As the advertisement said at the time, 'Go well go Shell'.

Chapter 3

IN THE TRACKS OF THE EIGHTH ARMY

Libya to Egypt

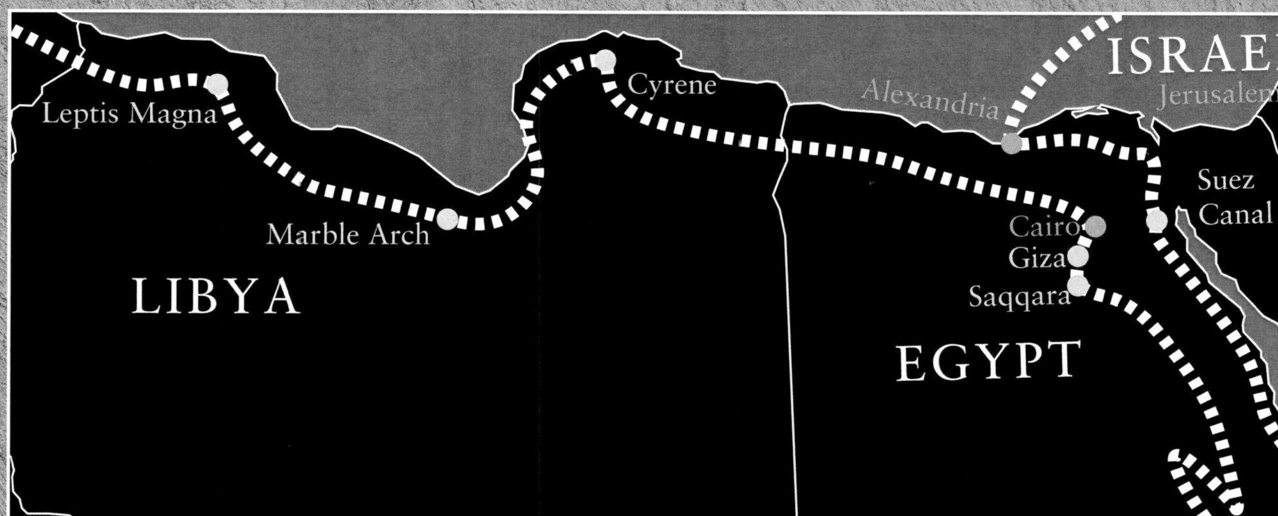

Leptis Magna

BY 6.30 A.M. the following morning, we had gone back by at least 2,000 years as we reached the incredible Roman city of Leptis Magna on the coast of Libya. Quite apart from the amazing historical vista, to me, it really did emphasise the whole point of forsaking what we both had in England and endorsed our decision to take the 'North African' route rather than the standard 'Hippy Trail' through Europe.

Here was an entire coastal Roman city, which in our estimation dwarfed Timgad. It is one of the best-preserved Roman ruins in the Mediterranean and, according to Gordon, far more impressive than Rome itself. You could walk entire wheel-rutted streets with shops and houses either side. The theatre is so close to the beach that there is a large channel behind the stage facilitating ships to literally sail through as the background of a performance. The acoustics of the theatre were uncanny, and as I sat on the highest row, I could quite clearly hear Gordon's voice from the stage. We were right back in history and almost had the city to ourselves, with no more than half a dozen locals wandering around.

Leptis Magna was founded in the 7th century BC and, in spite of an attempt by the Greeks to conquer it, remained an independent city. Like Timgad, it was surrounded by fertile farmland, and its core income came from the production of olive oil. Such was the growth of this industry, Caesar levied a tax on its production, and it became, with its seaport, a centre for Italian merchants.

Colonnades, basilica, amphitheatre, port, gymnasium, market place, theatre – an entire sun-dappled seaside city. Absolutely awesome, and one of the key sites of our journey.

Gymnasium, Leptis Magna

Leptis Magna

Front of the old Forum

Rear of the old Forum

General view of the Forum

Front of the Basilica, Leptis Magna

View beyond theatre toward Mediterranean sea

Note: channel behind theatre stage for floating ship backdrops

Theatre from the stage. Gordon in foreground immortalised?

Theatre

Baths

Gymnasium

Gymnasium

In a rather anti-climatic mood, we continued across very barren, arid scrubland and near Sirte plunged into the chilly sea for a refreshing swim. According to the AA, we would then come to the real desert that everyone reads about and visualises: great dunes of shifting yellow sand, stretching ridge after ridge to an endless horizon peppered with clear waterholes and oases shaded by palm trees. Not so. The Libyan desert turned out to be just hot, monotonous, flat, endless scrubland. We stopped for the night with just a few nomadic Arabs and the stars for company.

Once the fuel level indicated less than half a tank, we were always on the lookout for a petrol station. As luck would have it, we pulled up at a nondescript, scruffy, two-pump 'garage' in a remote village and asked the enthusiastic attendant if he would please fill up the car. The fuelling system wasn't mechanical but pumped by a long-handled lever. After a while, the Arab attendant's face changed from smiling enthusiasm to worried concern and the pace of his pumping slowed down. He couldn't understand where the petrol was disappearing to, so he stopped and looked around and under the Land Rover, sniffing and searching for a tell-tale puddle of fuel, to no avail! Totally nonplussed and confused, he continued his inspection until we took a turn at pumping. Eventually we were full, which engendered another look of confusion, as the counter indicated probably nearly a year's takings! With grins and handshakes all round, we set off towards Benghazi. This was once the assembly point for Rommel's forces and the target for an heroic Long Range Desert Group/SAS land attack in conjunction with a supporting naval one, which sadly ended in failure due to overwhelming opposition. However, it was recaptured by the Eighth Army in November 1941. Thus we were now in the zone of the British Eighth Army and German Afrika Korps theatre of war, where there were still remnants of this pivotal WW2 campaign, with many small shelters and dwellings built from abandoned jerry cans and destroyed armour. Our thoughts of further investigation to the south into the Sahara proper were quashed when we heard of two Australians killed by an exposed mine in the constantly wind-assisted shifting sands.

In 1937, the Italians built the 31-metre-high Arch of the Philaeni over the one single road along the north coast on the Cyrenaica/Tripolitania border. In due course, with the presence of many British troops, it inevitably became known as Marble Arch. In 1973 it was demolished by the Libyan dictator Colonel Muammar Gaddafi, who did not approve of a reminder of Italian colonisation. Ironic: one dictator, Benito Mussolini, had gone to Libya for the opening of the Arch, followed by another who destroyed it. Both of them destined for a sticky end.

Whilst in Benghazi, searching for some new shock-absorber bushes and engine mounts, we met a friendly group of somewhat chaotic Australians and New Zealanders. They were a bit surprised at our progress as we had reached there in half the time of their Bedford lorry, having covered the 4,200 miles from London in 11 days. Of course, the agent had every part but the items we needed, so we repaired to the nearby REME Officers Mess for some much-contemplated alcoholic refreshment and resolved to resume our parts search in Cairo.

'Marble Arch', Cyrenaica

However, we were given our marching orders by a seedy, gin-riddled major and decided to find camp as close as we could to the sea, some twenty miles further on, where we enjoyed a feast of chicken noodle soup, baked beans, corned beef and mugs of tea.

The next day was spent fettling and tidying the Land Rover before heading into Egypt. It took four hours just to replace the front offside oil seal, with Gordon's Land Rover tuition and mechanical expertise fully coming into play. By mid-afternoon, in addition to the seal, we had drained the axle, cleaned the air filter, bled and adjusted the brakes and repaired an exhaust leak. The bedding was aired and clothes-washing done, aided by our 'Tide'-donated washing powder. Another sort of tide and some Mediterranean salt eventually converted us back to the colour we had left England in.

We had heard that there was a possible fee if you attempted to get through the Egyptian border after 1.00 p.m., so we made a 6.00 a.m. start. This good intention was thwarted, as we took note of the Michelin map advising that the ruins of Tolmeor were '*très intéressantes*'. Not so! However, Cyrene was a different story altogether. Even today, it is noted as being rarely explored by tourists. It was originally a Greek settlement from 2500 BC and notably called the Athens of North Africa but then the Greeks were superseded by the Romans. It boasts one of the most impressive complexes of ruins in the world, rich in columns, temples, fountains, a working aqueduct, mosaics and a huge theatre. The students of Socrates established a school here and with the abundance of water coupled to an intricate irrigation system Cyrene became self-sufficient.

Cyrene

Cyrene, outer wall of Forum

Main Forum

Greek statues

Tombs

After lunch, we made for Derna on the coast, followed by a long, dull stint to Tobruk, another historic WW2 battle site, famed for the birth of the nomenclature 'Desert Rats' and the eight-week heroic defence in the summer of 1941 by General Morshead and his Australian troops. Their stand bought the Allies vital time and held on under constant bombardment until relieved by the Eighth Army, supported by the RAF and the Navy shipping in vital supplies. We stopped there for supper and then in the dark pushed on for another 70 miles.

We found Libya the most sociable of the North African countries, with the local Arabs sometimes giving help on the car or presenting us with a valued miniature 'chicken' egg. Maybe there was an ulterior motive with the ever-present 'baksheesh' demand, but none of it was malicious, and of course a few Rothmans produced huge smiles of appreciation. Although, in some cases, the filter tips caused consternation, as being unknown to the locals, they tried to light them up at the wrong end.

Besides being in Arabic the paucity of signposts was very apparent, but at least if we kept the Mediterranean on our left we couldn't go far wrong! Policemen were happy to try and help, but their English, understandably, was about as good as our Arabic. The latter were keen on their so-called 'checks' across the road, which were basically an excuse to interrogate the driver and demand money, but more than once we were able to slot into a 'convoy' (not least a British Army one) and avoid this expense.

You had to concentrate on the driving, which sometimes was hard, with long, featureless stretches of road. Arabs, goats, drifting sands, sheep and above all, another vehicle heading straight at you: these were constant distractions and reminders to focus on the driving.

The Libyan/Egyptian border crossing was interminable, but we knew we had better get used to it. It was a good thing we hadn't attempted it, in spite of the cost, late the previous day. Both countries had three different checkpoints, each separated by a few hundred yards. The process of crossing into Egypt took over two hours, and even then there were regular stops by the police to check the locals for tax and correct Egyptian number plates.

The time we had hoped to gain was lost, not least through the complete lack of signposts. We decided to abandon the proximity of the coastal route to Alexandria and take the direct 'express' road into Cairo, but by doing so, we inadvertently by-passed the site of the Battle of El Alamein, 60 miles west of the Egyptian capital. This crucial Allied victory there marked the end of the North African campaign and a turning point in WW2.

We stopped for a meal before completing the final 150 miles to the capital. However, as I was cranking open a tin of sardines with a pair of pliers, a very affable, English-speaking Egyptian pulled up and persuaded us to join him and a group of scouts at a nearby campsite. Initially we were rather reluctant to join in the festivities as we were pretty tired but eventually gave in, on the understanding that we must leave for Cairo by 6.00 a.m. the following morning. They had established a great camp-site, and soon a party was in full swing, where we experienced our first Egyptian outdoor meal. This was followed by singing, the Twist, Paso Doble and animated discussions on the merits or otherwise of President Nasser (known as Jimmy!), the Israeli situation (ongoing) and, somehow, a visit to/by the Chief of Police (also affable) – all lubricated with many cups of black tea. Quite a contrast and a very enjoyable one to our previous three weeks of isolated journeying.

We turned in at 4.30 a.m. and seemingly very shortly afterwards were persuaded by Nabil (our host) to visit his home in Alexandria, which we reached by 1.00 p.m. After lunch, he became our guide of his home town, which I have to say could only be described in one word… 'filthy' – and we will leave it at that! The generosity he and his parents showed us was overwhelming, and if ever we mentioned continuing to Cairo, it seemed as if it would bring on a seizure, they were so keen to host us. Much was planned but nothing constructive progressed, which we were soon to realise was the norm for the Egyptian way of life. Imagine the head of the household returning from work at 2.00 p.m. and then sitting around in the house in his pyjamas. But then 'pyjamas' seemed the standard daytime wear for all the men. In fact, not so bizarre, as pyjamas originated as sleep and lounge wear in India and consequently was more allied to hot climes.

After breakfast we had to complete more paperwork and, thanks to Nabil's contacts, were able to finalise the quadruple immigration forms at his local police station.

After visiting Pompey's Pillar and the especially opened University Museum, where we had our first sight of Egyptian relics, we set off to the teeming Egyptian capital of Cairo, famed city of a thousand minarets, via the 'express' route. Ironically, this stretch went through what we interpreted as real desert. We didn't reach Giza until after dark, but we parked in sight of the pyramids, which we hoped would remain standing for at least one more night!

Within a month, we had passed through cultures, civilisations, battlefields and history of which previously we had little conception. Motor sport and previous personal ambitions had paled into insignificance. We were now in a land going back millennia, with more history per square populated metre than any other country in the world.

By now we were becoming hardened to the constant begging. We were not averse to recompense when needed, but the repeated 'I need something for nothing' pleas could get very irritating. We eventually discovered that by turning around the request and holding one's hand out saying, 'No – baksheesh for me?' did put a lot of them off. If ever we left the car, you could guarantee on return there would be someone standing beside it requesting payment, as he had supposedly been guarding it diligently in our absence!

The pyramids being one of the world's major tourist attractions, there was a constant throng of hawkers offering rides on camels, horses and souvenirs, all of which we declined. However, the purveyors of these delights were soon mollified by a horde of very loud Americans in pseudo-tartan caps yelling, 'See you later, alligator!' I swear I saw the Sphinx roll his eyes in disgust!

Sphinx, Giza

Sphinx & Khufu pyramid

Sphinx from the other side

Pyramid of Khafre on left, Pyramid of Menkaure on right

Start of the climb to the top. 'Highlight' of the trip (pun intended)

We found a guide who agreed to take us to the top of the 480-ft-high Cheops Pyramid. This was hard work, literally clambering up the stone blocks and not helped by my complete lack of a head for heights, so not a good idea to look down until reaching the summit, which was a square area of stone blocks. Having reached the top, one was afforded one of the most moving and historical views one could experience, coupled with the awe and recognition of what those remarkable engineers had achieved. Surely the ultimate feat of manpower, which was a life's work for the majority of the artisans but in many instances then considered an honour!

The Pyramids at Giza must surely rank as one of mankind's greatest feats of engineering and are without compare. The impact of the achievement, without any modern technical aids but solely relying on manpower, is, in every sense, totally awesome.

Of the three pyramids, the largest, or Great Pyramid, is dedicated to Khufu or, by another name, Cheops. The others are called Khafre and Menkaure. They were built 4,500 years ago, starting in 2600 BC. It took 2.5 million stone blocks weighing a total of 6,000,000 tons, most of which were shipped up from Wadi al Jarf, 150 miles upstream on the Nile. An average three-monthly rota of 100,000 labourers toiled just to bring the stone to the building site. This was in direct contrast to those who were building the actual pyramids; they were respected and in the main freemen, working in shifts of 20,000. Then on arrival at a basin port the stones were unloaded and transported by camel direct to the site, having been shipped down a specially built connecting canal. From there, the stones were dragged by workers on wooden sledges over the sand to the building site.

On arrival at the site, the stones had to be carved both horizontally and vertically: the vertical to an exact angle of 51.8 degrees! The majority of the tools used were made from copper extracted from the Sinai peninsula. Once all the major blocks were in place, they were covered by an outer layer of 170,000 tons of limestone. No less than 68,000 of these casing stones were carved and, when in place, had minimal gaps. A lot of this outer layer covering was removed by Napoleon Bonaparte's troops for souvenirs. Ever ambitious, Napoleon instructed his engineers to dismantle a pyramid, but they very quickly gave up!

Pyramid of Khafre

'A magnificent view' would be an understatement. To the south, the Step Pyramid of Saqqarah and the Nile beyond, west to the other pyramids and desert, to the north desert and to the east, the teeming capital of Cairo. A spectacle burnished in the memory.

We took a photo of our Arab guide reading my previous employers' publication *Autosport*. A unique advertising opportunity, which was later declined, and a somewhat tempting expenses claim potential – 5000 miles at 9d a mile plus entertainment!

Descending, to the amazement of several onlookers, demanded concentration, as one slip could have resulted in more than an Elastoplast. Then, in direct contrast to the invigorating freshness of our climb, we entered the claustrophobic passage to the centre of the Cheops pyramid. In the centre are both the King's and Queen's chambers, 47 metres in length and 8 metres high. Surrounding the King's chamber are fire 'voids' or spaces around it to avoid collapse. Once a year, the head of the sarcophagus is symmetrically lit by a tiny light-filled channel from the top. To traverse this passage, we were bent double and the atmosphere was foetid, but again, the sight of the engineering accuracy and ingenuity fully justified the effort. A truly memorable and privileged experience which, to this day, leaves me in wonder.

Looking down at stone quarries

View south. Note: Sphinx

East towards Cairo

Chapter 4

AWESOME HISTORY

Egypt

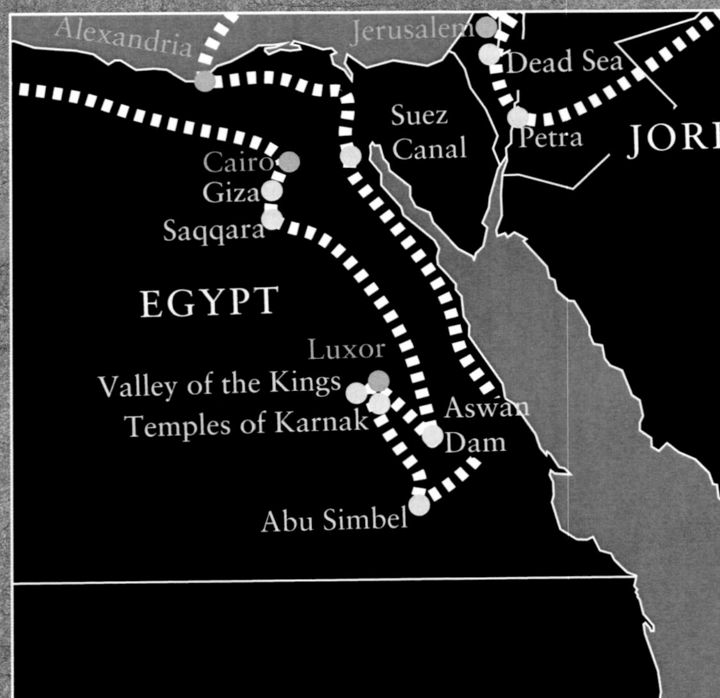

Egyptian Minister of Saqqara

By way of contrast to the last 5000 miles or so we were now back in the brash modern world and we set off on the short drive to Cairo. Our first call was to the American Express office to collect any mail and then to the Land Rover agents for a new oil seal, engine mounts and shock absorber bushes. Our plan was to cross the Sinai desert from Cairo and visit St Catherine's monastery, but this required a permit only obtainable from the Ministry of the Interior. After the fifth building we visited, we were advised the actual one we needed would not be open until 8.30 a.m. the following morning. So without more ado, we left the city and drove to Saqqara to view the tombs of Ta Holep and the minister Mererora. The stepped pyramid of Djoser is the earliest example of one built on this format by King Zoser in 2780 BC.

The site served as a necropolis of over 3000 years for Egypt's ancient capital Memphis. It is the oldest stone building complex in history. It is also the site of an extensive animal cemetery, many of which were regarded as sacred, such as cats, dogs, jackals and baboons. Also buried there are 24 mummified bulls placed in granite coffins, each weighing 15 tons!

We then treated ourselves to a mixed (very mixed!) grill at the 'Giza Casino' and returned to our camp site of the previous night. What a day: from 2780 BC to 1964 AD; the awesome achievements at Giza to the smog-filled, chaotic streets of modern Cairo!

The oldest 'step' Pyramid, Saqqara

Minarets for the call to prayer, Cairo

Above and right: Minarets for the call to prayer, Cairo

Cairo does not have a 'rush hour' as this is a permanent feature of one long chaotic, enervating, screaming, horn-blowing, stimulating dodgem ride. It made the first lap down Paddock Hill bend at Brands Hatch feel pretty tame in comparison, and we were glad we had our 'kangaroo bar' protection, which luckily wasn't required other than possibly (!?) as a collision deterrent. Eventually we reached the 'Sinai Embassy' and were told in no uncertain terms we could NOT drive direct to Aqaba. Further, if we wished to visit the monastery we would have to fill in endless forms and wait indefinitely in Cairo in the hopes we might get eventual, seemingly doubtful permission. We concluded this proposal was too open-ended and therefore elected to find passage to Lebanon from either Port Said or Suez.

From Lake Victoria to the Mediterranean Sea, the Nile is the longest river on Earth at 4130 miles

Such were the 'frosty' (to say the least) 'relations' between Egypt and Israel that attempting to cross their shared border would be futile. This situation could be further exacerbated if either country even found the opposite's stamp in a passport; you could be refused entry. This 'animosity' originated from the 1948 Arab-Israeli conflict over Palestine. With the bureaucracy behind us, we headed off for more history, which we found in the Cairo Museum. We spent several hours there viewing the series of incredible treasures and old filigree-encrusted sarcophagi. The wonderful hubbub of the street market and a visit to the gigantic Muhammed Ali Mosque, in the centre of the Muslim quarter, said to be a replica of the Blue Mosque in Istanbul, were our final stops before leaving the city. Throughout this throbbing metropolis there was a constant hubbub of chatter, bargaining and complaining from street hawkers, shopkeepers and calls to worship. The occasional 'military' sentries would have given a British Army CSM heart failure, clad in button-missing 'uniform' and with bolts missing from their rifles.

We headed south, feeling that if we kept the Nile on our right we should be OK; after all, there was only one 'main' road. Having said that, it was sometimes difficult to see which way the road turned, as it was a turbulent melange of Arabs, geese, camels, oxen, children, hens, goats, mangy dogs, sheep, chickens and poor donkeys scarcely visible under mountainous loads of heart-wrenching weight. Throughout the journey we witnessed unspeakable cruelty to animals, but it was futile to protest as there was nothing we could do. It is said the donkey is doomed to a life of persecution as it was ridden by Christ.

Timeless barges and feluccas

Sad sight of a mobile haystack

The car horn was nearly worn out and after 200 miles we pulled up at a very pleasant, quiet spot shaded by a palm grove. Soon we were hemmed in by some menacing locals brandishing rifles and machetes, who insisted we should follow them to the local police station. We managed to stave them off until after supper and then, on the pretence of following them, whizzed off down the road. After a few miles, we parked up again and turned in for the night. We had hardly gone to sleep when there was a violent knocking on the side of the Land Rover. It was the police insisting we move on, as the area was considered unsafe, especially for naïve, vulnerable tourists. Thus, bleary-eyed and with me just in my underpants, we followed them to the local gendarmerie, where we spent the rest of the night surrounded by Arabs armed with rifles and submachine guns!

We awoke to find ourselves surrounded again by a large crowd of curious, surly onlookers, so without further ado we didn't even leave the car and drove at the crowd, which opened like Moses' Red Sea, to find a calmer venue for breakfast.

Eighty miles short of Luxor, the term 'road' became debatable, with a mix of worn tarmac and potholes all enveloped by a choking dust. By contrast the Nile, dutifully ignoring the modern world, calmly proceeded north, bearing a serene traffic of tourist steamers, barges and feluccas. So slow was our progress that when reduced to walking pace it gave the opportunity for unwelcome passengers to hang on or climb onto the Land Rover.

Standard traffic chaos

Initial Aswan Dam construction

Endless diggings for the Aswan Dam

This problem was resolved by sharp acceleration, followed by sudden braking! Not that friendly, I admit, but we couldn't risk damage or accidents. The crush of people on this so-called highway was almost claustrophobic and for any stop, especially to eat, we ensured we locked ourselves in the car. Even then, we were continually cajoled for food, baksheesh, anything.

South of Luxor is the site of the vast, Russian-built Aswan Dam, which in time would result in Lake Nasser becoming the largest man-made 'lake' in the world, measuring some 340 miles long. Thus huge canals and irrigation channels north of Luxor were being built in a spider's web of construction. The Egyptian President, Colonel Gamel Abdel Nasser, had deposed the indolent King Farouk in 1952. Shortly after the coup, with the objective of raising Egypt's prestige – and not least to control the disruptive flooding of the Nile's water in times of drought to the key crop-growing areas of the lower Nile and the Nile Delta – Nasser approached the British and Americans to help finance the dam, to which they agreed. Such is the fertility of the Nile (the name derived from the Greek, meaning river) that it supports over 90% of the nation whilst only covering a twentieth of it! However, in 1956 these countries withdrew their funding, prompting Colonel Nasser to nationalise the Suez Canal and thus use its profits to fund the dam's construction. At this point the USSR stepped in, offering both financial and technical assistance to what was to become one of the largest embankment dams in the world. It took ten years to build, and work commenced in 1960. This accounted for the never-ending crowds of workers, who camped locally and otherwise were digging and dumping soil with seemingly haphazard abandon. However, certainly with the Russians involved, there was a plan somewhere to oversee this modern-day human ant's nest of endeavour. The completed dam is 4000 metres long, 980 metres high and 40 metres wide at its base.

We were just ahead of two other distinguished visitors, namely the aforesaid Colonel Nasser and the Russian leader Nikita Khrushchev, who arrived on the 14th May to divert the Nile so construction could progress.

Our 400 miles of motoring from Cairo to Luxor literally transported us through time, and the world we had left was long-forgotten. We did consider sending postcards, but the price of stamps and our obvious scepticism of their reaching the intended recipients precluded such communications. We topped up with fuel and water and bought some supper from one of the many stalls in the town, then found a 'presumed quiet' spot to camp on the banks of the Nile.

Ram headed sphinx, Karnak, Luxor

Luxor, on the East bank, is the site of the ancient capital of Upper Egypt, namely Thebes, founded in approximately 1400 BC. It became a centre of social prestige, expensive luxury and the trappings of resident domineering politicians. Undoubtedly this river bridgehead in time became second to Angkor Wat in Cambodia as the largest religious site in the world. It is spread over a complex of four main areas, but only one area was open to the public. The most impressive aspects of the Temple of Karnak are the size and scale of the monuments and buildings, some of which in due course were to form a backdrop in a James Bond film – perhaps not the best recommendation!

Aman-Re temple

The most famous area is the 50,000 square foot Hypostyle Hall, which features 134 ten-metre columns in sixteen rows. The architraves atop these sandstone columns weigh 70 tons. On the walls of the Hall are reliefs depicting the conquest of a rebellion against Ramses II. Behind the hall is the Sacred Lake overlooked by one of the many of ancient, revered Egyptian motifs – the Scarab beetle.

The Sacred Lake with scarab, in the precinct of Aman-Re

Karnak. The precinct of temples and chapels cover 2.5 sq km

King Ramses II

Hypostyle hall

Tempie of Karnak, Luxor

First pylon of the Aman-Re temple

Aman-Re temple

A short walk down the bank of the Nile and across on a ferry to another history lesson. We were confronted by two massive sandstone statues, each 18 metres high and weighing 720 tons each. These are of a seated King Amenhotep III and were built in 1350 BC. They are known as the Colossi of Memnon and were named as a result of one of the statues making noises or 'singing'. The theory of this is that the right statue was split by an earthquake and when the wind blows through the cracks 'a song' is heard which, in due course, was believed to be 'oracles' in the form of the goddess Eos mourning the death of her son, Memnon. Memnon was an Ethiopian king who was killed by a no less famous warrior, Achilles, in the Trojan wars. Thus the statues became known as the Colossi of Memnon.

The enthusiasm of the locals on reaching the opposite bank made the sales patter of an East London car salesman seem amateur, but in this instance it was for the hire of four legs not four wheels. We were feeling somewhat sorry for these luckless beasts of burden but the sun was blazing, so practicality overruled sympathy, and after cost-reducing negotiations we set off on the nine-kilometre journey to the Valley of the Kings.

Colossi of Memnon, on the west bank of the Nile

The hill route to the Valley of the Kings with the Nile in the distance

The tombs are set in twin valleys in the Theban hills, and both animals and ourselves were very pleased to get there after a very hot hour's saddle-sore journey. These world-famous tombs were excavated over a period of 500 years from the 16th century BC. In the majority of cases it was only kings or queens who were afforded such tombs and sometimes, to a much lesser degree, a nobleman or very important politician. The Ancient Egyptians believed in the afterlife and were thus entombed firstly in a series of sarcophagi, like Russian dolls, and surrounded by all they needed, including their closest servants and courtiers, who considered in an honour to pass to the next life with their pharaoh. The tombs were filled with a vast treasure trove of gold-encrusted-filigree chariots, jewellery, furniture and everything they considered they would need in the new life. The riches and treasures they contained have long been removed, either plundered by thieves or, particularly latterly, for vital preservation at museums throughout the world – not least, appropriately, in major displays in Cairo.

Legend has it that anyone violating and opening one of these tombs would be cursed. Nonetheless, Lord Carnarvon, the sponsor of Howard Carter – who discovered the most famous tomb, that of the nineteen-year-old pharaoh king Tutankhamun in 1922 – was allowed to take a small collection of artefacts which are housed in a downstairs room near the kitchens of his descendants' home, Highclere Castle (or perhaps now better known to some as 'Downton Abbey'!).

Tomb entrance in the Valley of the Kings

The tomb of King Tutankhamun

Sarcophagus of King Tutankhamun

We visited the tombs of Ramses VI, Seti I and Amenophis II, but not surprisingly it was the tomb of King Tut, as he became known in the modern world, that even today was clearly the most ornate. One descended a long, steep flight of steps, at the same angle as accessing a London tube station, but instead of poster advertisements on either side were a tableau of colourful hieroglyphics telling the story of the life of the king entombed below. At the bottom of the stairs was an open chamber, again with exceptionally well preserved hieroglyphics on the walls and ceiling. In the middle was the outer stone sarcophagi of King Tutankhamun. Photography was restricted, but nonetheless a truly memorable experience.

Hieroglyphics on tomb entrance

We took our guide's advice of a shorter route back to the ferry. This proved to be on a narrow track on the edge of the hills, which didn't help my vertigo. Added to this, my donkey developed a limp on the rear offside and Gordon's donkey had diarrhoea.

Thus we were somewhat relieved, together with the donkeys, to return to the Colossi, where just to the north of us some American archaeologists were overseeing the rebuilding of the vast Mortuary Temple of Queen Hatshepsut.

Hieroglyphics depicting voyage to the afterlife

Brave donkeys and passengers

View down onto the Temple of Queen Hatshepsut

Temple of Queen Hatshepsut

Later that day, having crossed the Nile back to Luxor, we set off south, leaving behind the vast avenues, columns and obelisks of the Karnak Temple on the 150-mile drive to Aswan. Aswan had achieved fame in colonial days with the famous Hotel Cataract, which was a favourite venue of Winston Churchill. The site overlooks the first series of the obstructive Nile cataracts whose narrows and islands caused huge problems in the 1880s for the General Gordon relief force pushing south to Khartoum, forcing them to land and haul their boats upriver, and not least depriving them of critical time. This was more of a track than a road, and for the first half we were crawling along then across desert to the luxury of the final forty miles of tarmac, courtesy of the Russians, and finally an overnight halt after a historically memorable day in every sense.

We had lost track of dates, so the next morning, being a Friday, the overwhelming priority for all was worship, and the air was filled with prayer and chanting. Another service check was due on the Land Rover after the battering it had taken in recent days. We found a relatively quiet spot and camped near a huge unfinished obelisk which had been hewed directly from the bedrock until cracks appeared in the granite and it was consequently abandoned on site. It is nearly a third bigger than any other Egyptian obelisk, measuring nearly 137 feet; if completed, it would have weighed 1200 tons.

Vital Land Rover servicing

The car's remaining front oil seal was changed and the shock absorber bushes (very important!) checked, as was the timing. We then drove to the construction site of the Aswan Dam to see for ourselves what was keeping some 12,000 Russians and countless Arabs so busy. The whole vast area was frenetic, with hundreds of lorries hurtling about dumping earth, debris and huge rocks. What had already been achieved was approaching the scale of endeavour we had seen of their forebears, but the projected completion date was another four years hence. (In fact, it took a further six.)

We needed to finalise the best means to get to Abu Simbel on the edge of the Nubian desert, another 150 miles further south. However, before we progressed this plan, we met two chaps who had been on the road for eight months and had covered a lot of our intended route. Thus in the middle of Egypt, amongst other things, we learned how to ship a car from Sri Lanka to Australia with the assistance of a black market agency in Colombo!

The alternatives of reaching Abu Simbel were to cross the desert with an expensive guide or to go it totally alone, which by all accounts could be categorised 'as really pushing one's luck'. Even so, the Land Rover was duly topped up with water, fuel and supplies. It was then discovered that we had a broken leaf in one of the rear springs, which immediately ruled out any cross-desert motoring and was probably just as well. Thus it would be the ferry, but its sailing was a week away, resulting in the closest Gordon and I ever came to any dissension, deciding whether it was worth waiting for. I am glad we did. During the afternoon we visited the Temple of Kalabsha, which had been totally dismantled at its original site and rebuilt like a jigsaw on higher ground above the projected level of the planned Lake Nasser.

Reliefs at the Temple of Kalabsha

We tried in vain to find passage to Abu Simbel on the locally moored steamers, tugs and barges before the Monday sailing but to no avail. The several possible alternatives were discussed and mulled over that evening in the company of two American hitchhikers and an Englishman in a very battered but comprehensively equipped VW combi. The next day we visited the offices of the Sudanese Railway Company in search of our boat booking. They, in turn, informed us these could only be obtained from the El Shallal railway station, from which we had been turned away the previous day! All fairly standard procedure in this part of the world, but it is pointless to get excited about it as to do so means a situation can rapidly progress from bad to worse! Then we were told you can only buy tickets on the day of the sailing. Thus we had a few days wait, which were spent mostly sunbathing, local site-seeing and double-checking every aspect of the Land Rover.

River traffic

Four vessels roped together for the ferry trip from Aswan to Wadi Halfa, Sudan

At last Monday arrived, with a scheduled sailing from the High Dam at 4.00 p.m. The morning was taken up with securing the Land Rover and packing our rucksacks for the trip as we had to be totally self-sufficient. We took our sleeping bags, a few medical supplies, two tins of peaches, corned beef, our stove, bread, tomatoes and some oranges, plus a large water container. The last bus left at noon for El Shellal and from there another to the boat. The main 'ferry', which provided the propulsion, was in the middle of a cluster of four boats roped together – a single barge to the stern and one each side. The leading boat had a row of cabins, an eating area, a roof and a loo. The other three were open to the elements and housed every shape, size and colour of both humans and livestock, excepting perhaps a camel. It was a heaving mass of activity, with constant chatter, clucking of chickens accompanied by an all-pervading aroma of cooking, bodies, noise and the smoking of dubious, exotic substances. It was a friendly and relaxed atmosphere and all considered in what we would regard discomfort in normal life. We were travelling deck class, which meant we had to scramble for a space on the deck and once found – to keep it. Your mat, rug, sleeping bag (rare) or simply an item of clothing marked your 'living quarters' for the trip. Men had to occupy the port deck and women the starboard. Eventually, some two and a half hours behind schedule, we sailed, or more accurately, 'burbled' off into the main channel of the placid Nile. At the appointed hour our fellow passengers prepared to pray, aligning their prayer mats towards Mecca and taking off some of their robes. In so doing they revealed an impressive array of concealed weaponry. A policeman advised us that stoves on deck were forbidden, so brewing took somewhat longer than usual as we had to watch for his return. A party of touring Egyptians very generously insisted we slept in their 2nd class 'cabin' and in spite of our protests we were eventually persuaded. Gordon won the toss for the bunk and I slept on the floor.

Daylight revealed the effect the Aswan Dam would have on the Nile, the waters of which had obviously risen appreciably already. There were many treetops just above the surface and lots of abandoned dwellings and villages, only the occasional felucca on a fishing trip giving any sign of habitation. We passed the Temple of Philae, site of the last examples of hieroglyphics, which was destined to be reduced to 37,000 pieces and rebuilt away from the projected flooding.

We arrived at Abu Simbel at 3.00 p.m. after a 22-hour voyage where the ferry moored for an hour before continuing upstream to Wadi Halfa, which is on the border of Egypt and the Sudan. As we disembarked, the ferry Captain kindly warned us of hostile locals, who had recently murdered a French tourist, and to beware of scorpions.

Steel for the coffer dam

The two temples of Abu Simbel, named after the young Bedouin guide of John Lewis Burckhardt (he anglicised his forenames), the Swiss explorer and discoverer of the site in 1813, were built in the reign of Ramses II (1279-1213 BC) on the original Egyptian/Nubian border. (Burckhardt was an impressive explorer and traveller who had previously made an illegal journey to Medina and Mecca disguised as a Muslim sheikh.) The temple took twenty years to build from 1265-1244 BC and was 'simply' cut 185 feet into the cliff.

Abu Simbel: boatload of steel being unloaded for the construction of the coffer dam prior to dissecting the temple and rebuilding it at the top of the cliff. (Note: The rising lake, which was destined to immerse the temple site.)

Front façade of main temple, Abu Simbel

Murals at the entrance of the temple

The four main 20-metre-high colossi of King Ramses wearing the double crown of Lower and Upper Egypt form the front façade with the entrance to the temple in the middle. One of the heads of the King had sheared off, damaged by an earthquake, and in between these colossi are statues of family members and conquered enemies. Through the main entrance we proceeded into a pillared hall 18 metres long with many reliefs and engravings of conquests and celebrations, to a smaller, four-pillared hall decorated with offerings to the Gods. The back wall of this second hall was so positioned that twice a year – February 22 and October 22 – the beams of the sun symmetrically light up these sculptures. It is suggested that these two dates commemorate the King's birthday and coronation, and the sun's timing was to give credence to King Ramses' claim that he was a God.

The rising Nile was only some 50 feet from the front of the temple. Nearby is a smaller version of the main temple – only the second time one was dedicated to a queen. The statues in this temple reach a height of 12 metres.

Worm's eye view of 70ft colossi of King Ramses

We reached these temples, in a sense just in time, as a succession of barges and cranes were busy unloading steel girders with which to build a coffer dam around them. Thus protected from the rising Nile waters, the temples could then be dismantled and reassembled on the cliffs above. This was a major UNESCO project incorporating the engineering experience and skills of the Swedes and the Germans, and the relocation was completed four years after our visit.

It was roasting and the sand so hot it was impossible to walk barefoot. In spite of the captain's warnings (not that we had any choice), we spent the night on the sand in front of the temple. In fact, I found a large, flat marble tombstone marking the grave of a British sergeant who was part of the Khartoum relief force of 1884/5. However, it seemed discourteous to sleep on this in spite of an apology and it was also very hard. No matter, for as we were preparing our 'dinner' and naively contemplating a night's sleep, we were suddenly aware of a thrumming akin to the London Symphony Orchestra tuning up. Far from musical but a large, dense, dark cloud of mosquitoes, no doubt contemplating us as their dinner. Predictably not much sleep was achieved. We rested with a torch close to hand not only for light but as a puny weapon with thoughts of the aforementioned local murderer. I suddenly awoke feeling breath on my neck and lashed out. The perceived 'murderer' was in fact a dog, who whimpered off to his master; both of them had seemingly materialised from nowhere and were encouraged to leave with curses and handfuls of sand.

Up with the dawn at the recommended time of sunrise, though temple viewing was marred by a horde of boat-moored, visiting German tourists in large straw hats. Most of the day was spent vainly trying to keep cool. It was frustrating not to take a plunge into the Nile, but we had been warned that in this area the lake, with little current, was subject to bilharzia, a virulent water-borne bug which attacks the stomach. We spent a long, hot day on the scorching sandy beach in front of the temple with the occasional sustenance of stale bread, tomatoes or an orange. After another sleepless night, spent this time within the cooler confines of the temple in a vain attempt to escape the unrelenting torture of the mosquitoes, the sunrise penetrated the dawn to gradually light up the temple corridor. Consequently, we could well imagine the excitement and awe of those witnessing the symmetrically lighting up of the altar on those two memorable days.

The sunrise penetrates the dawn to gradually light up the temple corridor

It was good to see 'our boat' again the following afternoon, since the night had been one constant mosquito-swatting exercise and we were feeling tired, hungry and unwashed. However, an international conference back on our deck class with some Germans, Americans and Australians, interspersed with surreptitious visits to the 'First Class' lounge for suitable refreshments, soon revived us! As we were disembarking, five hours behind schedule, at the Aswan Dam there was a sudden, unexpected demand for vaccination certificates, which caused consternation in some quarters but luckily not in ours, as one of our many cocktail jabs in London qualified us. A few piastres and collective encouragement persuaded our bus driver to keep going from El Shellal to 'our home' – the Land Rover at Aswan, which we were surprised and pleased to find intact! We had a quick meal of beans, corned beef and pickles before setting off north … destination Suez. We kept parallel with the Nile for a while and, after saying goodbye to this legendary river, headed east towards the Red Sea, or Mare Erythraeum, to give it its Latin name. After our previous sleep-deprived night, we decided to stop early and continue on at dawn. We crossed the hilly, sandy scrubland of the eastern desert and were relieved to note we had not met any of the rumoured active bandits of that area who had a penchant for robbing travellers. The only signs of habitation we saw were small desolate townships – ideal backdrops for a spaghetti western – and tented military encampments. We crested a hill and there in the distance was the azure blue, white and green vista of the Red Sea, which was an uplifting contrast to the heat, sand and dust of the past few weeks. We bought some eggs at Port Safaga in the market place for a roadside lunch. Then we headed up the coast, aiming for Suez with the intention of having a swim in the Red Sea, but whilst admiring the coral we spotted a shark so quickly got out.

Latterly our progress was slowed by a very poor road and our complaining broken leaf spring. We had hoped naively we could research a boat to Aqaba or more likely, Beirut, but the only possibility had left the previous day. So we continued north to Ismailia, equidistant from Suez and Port Said, in the hopes that enquiries there would prove more fruitful and thus avoid us taking on Port Said. We had done well and covered a little short of 500 miles. Diligent enquiries as to shipping possibilities in Ismailia proved fruitless, so we had no choice but to continue north to Port Said. Here, as we were both looking a bit shaggy, we decided to have a haircut. There was a lot of 'anti-British sentiment' in the area (nothing new there!), and with the increasing tension with Israel, not helped by their water-diverting scheme, we were somewhat on our guard. Thus, after his haircut, when Gordon felt a sharp blow on the back of his neck he shot out of the chair, to the startled barber's amazement, but he was only apparently giving Gordon a neck massage. Shopping for food supplies had its drawbacks, as we were not adequately equipped for properly cleaning our purchases. This caught up with me in no uncertain terms in Port Said, necessitating a dip into the medical supplies. Otherwise in Egypt we enjoyed a cheap diet of vegetables and fruit, particularly oranges, to supplement our own basic supplies. For a change the road was tarmac and dead straight, running parallel with the Suez Canal on our right with its ships floating serenely past just like clouds in the sky.

Chapter 5

RICH AND POOR

Lebanon and Syria

IN SPITE OF a puncture – hard work with heavy-treaded tyres, requiring several levers to remove them from the wheel – we made good time, and a travel agency advised us there was a sailing from Alexandria to Beirut in three days. Progress! Our previous host, Nabil, had generously insisted we return to Alexandria so at least a timetable seemed to be falling into place. We doubled back to Ismailia and crossed the fertile Nile delta area via Tanta to Alexandria, getting there at dusk. Nabil and his very hospitable family were so pleased to see us that they took us out to dinner and on top of this introduced us to a friend who insisted we stay in his seaside villa. Thus we found ourselves in our own quarters including bedroom, dining room, kitchen and – total luxury – running water, situated two minutes from the sea! As luck would have it, we had emptied the contents of the Land Rover prior to an overhaul and complete spring clean. The following morning we met Nabil at the University faculty, where we were the centre of attention of many students who were keen to meet Westerners. Then to the tourist agency to try and obtain the elusive sailing tickets to Lebanon. We had just missed a Turkish boat sailing the same afternoon, but it was too late to catch it. What was the hurry, anyway? I can't answer that! Nabil's help and patience were invaluable, as the agency seemed to have a philosophy of making everything as complicated as possible. This trend got worse as the day progressed and in spite of the firm resolve by Egyptians in the morning to get everything done that day, invariably by the evening very little was achieved. Thanks, though, to Nabil's assistance we booked and paid for our tickets to sail in three days' time. The evening's highlight was a visit to a local night club where we were inundated with food and the promise of 'the best belly dancer in all of Egypt'. We awaited the cabaret with an anticipation of loveliness, scantily performing erotic manoeuvres from the waist down in a blur of mysticism. Sadly, when this temptress eventually appeared she was obviously a matron of many summers who tumbled her fat belly, which, without any encouragement from her, wobbled vertically, contrary to the 'Strictly Come Dancing' handbook.

The following morning gave us a chance to clean out the Land Rover, buy some provisions and write some letters (relations were probably wondering where we were!) before Farouk, the owner of the villa, took us out to a fantastic lunch at one of Alexandria's most exclusive restaurants. Then tea with more Egyptian friends, followed by a tour of Alexandria guided by Nabil. Late nights, late starts, a bed, a bath, endless food were all taking some getting used to after our previous routine.

The next day did not start well, as we were woken by a small boy who beckoned us to the Land Rover parked outside. The rear window had been prised open, and tins of food and some belongings were strewn across the road. The inside had been ransacked and everything gone through. Cameras, lenses, light meter and a stopwatches were gone, but luckily our vital papers such as carnet and passports were safe in their padlocked container under the passenger seat. Our fault, as we should have taken everything into the house. We had heard that all thefts must be reported to the police, and although sceptical about this as we didn't think for a minute our belongings would be returned, if we did report it then there was more chance of getting some insurance recompense. We all know how naïve that thought is, but nonetheless eventually two very bored, nut-chewing, tea-drinking constables arrived to take the details. No one seemed the slightest bit interested or made any real effort to assist, but we were in another country in another culture, so there was little point in pursuing the matter. We thus resolved to get new cameras in Beirut, though we could ill afford such expenditure. This incident did encourage us to move on as soon as possible but we didn't want to appear ungracious after such generous hospitality, and besides we had booked the boat that was 'rumoured' to sail the following afternoon.

The S/S Nedia was scheduled to depart to Beirut at 3.00 p.m., which necessitated our being at Customs by noon. After a needless rush to clean our villa and repack the Land Rover, the booking agency phoned Nabil to advise us that the boat was delayed and we didn't need to get to Customs until 3.30 p.m. This delay was welcome as it gave us a chance to properly thank Nabil and his family for their generosity and insight into the Egyptian way of life. We got to the docks on schedule but no one knew where the Customs were based! Then we were told we couldn't enter the docks before 7.00 p.m! Back to the booking agency: 'No, no you MUST be there by 5.00 p.m.' Returning to the docks where we eventually found Customs, we were told that the Nedia hadn't even docked! The whole rigmarole repeated itself that evening with endless paperwork in triplicate and passports hammered with stamps and hieroglyphics. The Nedia finally docked at 10.00 p.m., and we were informed at midnight that the dockers refused to load us until the following morning, so we turned in for the night in the car.

Next morning the foreman advised us he had to be paid to load our car in spite of the agency's assurance all was included. He wasn't going to load the car and we hadn't the extra money to pay him as it was our policy, when leaving a country, that we would spend all our remaining local currency to top up with fuel. The cars were loaded by slinging then onto a net and then craning them all aboard, so Gordon and I set about jacking the car up to slip the net under the wheels one axle at a time. This sent the spectating dockers into paroxysms of mirth as we attached the net to the crane hook. Of course, what we should have done was simply to drive the car onto the net. Such entertainment broke the ice, and the crane driver promptly jumped into his cab and winched the car aboard. Just as well, as I think we might have struggled to operate the crane! As we finally headed out to a rough Mediterranean sea we watched the liner of its day, the white-hulled Canberra, heading for Australia and concluded we were better travelling overland.

Our voyage took nineteen hours, but in contrast to the Egyptian border crossings we were soon through the Lebanese Customs. However, being a Sunday next day, all offices and shops were closed, so we camped on the beach. Sunday, as for most, was an enforced (for us) rest day and with our first real rain storm we headed for the cinema to watch Sonny Liston vs Cassius Clay and a Norman Wisdom film – and we had come all the way from London for this! The overall impression of Beirut – which was not unlike the Cote d'Azure, with large houses, big American cars and British sports cars, not least Jaguars – was an enclave of wealth and luxurious living. You were either very rich or very poor, with a financial gulf in between. As ever that was on the volatile surface of daily life but in due course drastically set to change.

We were in the city early the next morning as we had yet to find a new leaf for our battered rear spring. After many recommendations and diversions we found a garage who fitted this while we waited as we hadn't the equipment to do it ourselves. We collected some mail and joined some students for lunch at the American University. As we were short of money, we were disappointed to learn at the local hospital that they didn't want to buy our blood (a normally popular source of income), which would have boosted our finances. I had been given the name of Captain Twite, a British European Airways pilot based near Beirut within the village of Baabda, so I phoned him, whereupon he very kindly invited us to stay. His home was in the hills amongst the famed cedar trees, with a panoramic view of the suburbs, the city and the sea. We made vain efforts at the airport to pass as transit passengers in order to get a cheaper 'duty-free' camera to no avail but eventually found an identical one to Gordon's previous one in the city. The Twites then drove us up the coast to one of the oldest towns in the world, Byblos. The name 'Byblos' comes from the Greek for papyrus, from which in turn the name 'Bible' derives (the 'papyrus book'). The town was once a key Phoenician port and has been continuously inhabited for over 7000 years. We had a quiet lunch on the quayside watching the fishermen tend their nets and set them out on a sparkling Mediterranean. The whole town was in need of some restoration, which nonetheless did not put off hordes of tourists, and if one eavesdropped on the guide's recital, we learned some of the history. With colour slides to sort and number and more unwelcome rain, we took a day 'off' and headed back to the city of Beirut, where we were told we would get the highest rates of exchange from the money changers. Their stalls took up a complete square, with the constant jabber of offers, deals and exchange rates: in fact, a non-pinstripe-suited version of the London Stock Exchange and just as frenetic. We exchanged our traveller's cheques for Syrian pounds, Jordanian dinars, Iranian rials, Pakistani and Indian rupees. Fortified with a nostalgic British breakfast, we left promptly the next morning on the Damascus road to the north. Gradually the stunning views of Beirut, the distant Mediterranean and the cedars faded as we continually climbed through an endless succession of hairpin bends. We then came into the 90-mile Bequaa valley, which is Lebanon's most fertile agricultural region in spite of receiving limited rainfall. It is the northern tip of the Great Rift Valley all the way up from East Africa and was flanked by imposing snow-covered mountains. It is also a major centre for drug production of hashish and opium, but we didn't stop to investigate such products!

Our tempers were tested when some two hours later we discovered we had left behind at the Twite residence Gordon's new wide-angle camera lens. However, all such frustrations were soon forgotten as we arrived at Baalbek, the ancient Phoenician 'City of the Sun'. It became an important pilgrimage site for the sky god Baal. Alexander the Great conquered it in 334 BC and the previously named Henopolis became the 'City of the Sun'. After Pompey's annexation, Baalbek became a Roman colony some 49 years later. The Romans, as ever, vastly improved the infrastructure, building many new roads and aqueducts.

Temple of Bacchus, Baalbek

Temple of Bacchus, Baalbek

Temple of Jupiter

Temple of Jupiter

The grand temple of Jupiter is the most ornate and largest religious building in the history of the Roman Empire, with its six remaining columns of 60 feet the highest in the ancient world. In more modern times, Baalbek was the venue where T. E. Lawrence ('Aurens', as the Arabs called him), whilst en route to an intelligence meeting in Damascus, met Arab nationalists to discuss opportunities for a local uprising. This brave and important foray – and not least his sabotage-led actions on Turkish communications and encampments, culminating with his victorious attack on Aqaba – earned him a recommendation for the Victoria Cross. However, this could not be endorsed, since no other British combatant was present to witness these actions and thus the proposed award was reduced to a DSO.

Baalbek dedicated to the god Baal, otherwise Zeus

Later, the French recommended Lawrence for a Croix de Guerre and for him to be made a Chevalier of the Legion d'Honneur, but again he declined and never even wore any of the attendant medal ribbons.

Ironically, the god Baal couldn't organise any sun for us, so we set off back to Baabda and the generous Twites to collect the missing camera lens. We turned down a kind offer of another night's stay and having retrieved the lens decided not to retrace our wheel tracks. We took the coast road north via Byblos – called by the Crusaders 'Gibeletto', or 'Giblet', as at that time the area was ruled by the Genoese Embriaco family – and then through Tripoli. More Customs questioning and hassles, but in fairness I don't suppose two itinerant Englishmen in a UK-registered Land Rover needing to cross the frontier were too frequent.

We stopped at Homs as instructed by the border guards to register with the police and headed for the historic medieval castle Krak des Chevaliers, some 30 miles to the East. T.E.L. nominated this castle as the most important example of its type in the world. He made a study of Near East crusader castles, and his resultant thesis on the subject won him a First with Honours at Oxford University. This thesis was eventually published in book form, complete with plans, maps and photos. Such skills were to serve Lawrence well, as his detailed charts, maps and topography expertise proved useful to the British military subsequently in Arabia.

It was a long climb up to the castle, and we frequently had to engage four-wheel drive, with the final muddy few kilometres being enveloped in mist. With dusk approaching, we parked in the lea of the gigantic battlements, eager to see what would be revealed in the morning.

Rain fell in torrents during the night, accompanied by thunder and lightning, so we were frustrated the next morning with the resultant drizzle and mist, rendering decent photography impossible. By the time we had completed our tour of this mighty fortification, we 'discovered' it had an inner ward and an outer ward built on a hilled site, which afforded steep defensive slopes on all sides except one. Originally it was a Kurdish garrison, but then it passed to the Knights Hospitaliers in 1142. It was finally abandoned in 1271, having eventually succumbed to a 36-day siege after many attacks. This was not, as in the case of many castles, an administrative centre but a prime fortification, at one point housing a garrison of nearly 2000. I spent a while using my military training to contemplate how this formidable fortification could be taken and was gratified to note when reading the castle's history that the route I had selected was in fact exactly the one that had been used to overcome it.

The castle guarded several of the mountain passes from the east Mediterranean coast and was the site of many battles and bloodshed as it was dedicated by the Crusaders to the defence

Krak des Chevaliers, Crusader castle

of the Holy Land. In modern times, the French undertook a lot of its restoration before it passed to Syrian jurisdiction when the country became independent in 1946. It dwarfed any other castle we had seen either in Britain or Europe, and on a clear day (not the one in the photographs) you can view the distant Mediterranean Sea. Coincidentally, whilst we were trying to discern a sea view an Arab approached us and kept pointing, saying what we thought was 'ships, ships'. We assumed he wanted to guide us around the castle and show us some representation of a fleet of ships, but it was not a tour and the 'ships' were in fact 'sheeps'! A truly spectacular visit to a cornerstone of Crusader history.

Outer ramparts

Gothic chapel

Within the castle walls looking west

Within the castle walls looking west

Back to our focal point of Homs and then another detour, this time some 200 miles, to the ancient, originally 200-acre settlement of Palmyra in the Syrian desert, which was founded in the third millennium BC. Palmyra, meaning 'city of palm trees' (although we didn't see a single one), achieved its prominence as a halfway 'oasis' between the Mediterranean sea and the Euphrates river. It was a key link to the Roman world and the east, becoming an important trading point on the Silk Road. The Emperor Hadrian subsequently declared it a 'free city' and then a later Roman emperor granted it exemption from taxes. However, with increasing instability in the region, not least the demise of their longstanding enemies the Parthians, the city was taken over by the Muslims in 634 AD.

The rain had returned but we splashed on through. It was nice to enjoy for once some green fields and small streams, only to find, to our disappointment, the main temple was closed. However, after a little reconnaissance we were able to parachute jump down into the forecourt. We had not come all this way to be barred from viewing such a key archaeological site! Again the light was bad, but we managed a few photographs. The ruins cover a huge area and in the distance overlooking the site was the remains of a large Arabic fort built on the crest of a hill. Perhaps we were getting somewhat blasé by now, just taking these amazing ruins for granted, but overall thus far Leptis Magna, in Libya, got our vote for its setting, state of preservation and unique remains of a complete city, including theatre, basilica, gym, etc.

Another major factor of our enjoyment of these visits was that as often as not we were the only visitors, and even when we were not alone, it was usually only curious nomadic locals with us, rarely hordes of noisy tourists. It must have been this factor that encouraged someone to shoot at us. There was a crack and a ricochet on a nearby rock so, not being fluent in the local patois, we thought it best to leave rather than register our disapproval. So we backtracked the 200 miles to Homs and enjoyed Mrs Twite's kind donation of Wall's pork sausages, bacon and eggs! (It is, of course, of grave concern that during the recent Syrian conflict both Krak des Chevaliers and Palmyra have been desecrated by IS forces.)

It was a pleasant change to wake up and note a clear blue sky, accompanied by the god Baal's warm contribution. The road to Damascus was beautiful, with small villages cradled in the shelter of low hills. We went through mountain passes and on to a flat, fertile plain. Many of the scenes we saw were as they had been for centuries; time had scarce moved on, dominated as the landscape was by Bedouin intently minding their meandering flocks of sheep.

Arch of Triumph, Palmyra, with Arab castle of Fakhr-Al-Din-Al-Maan on hill crest

Temple of Bel. Palmyra has the largest and best preserved temple complex in the world (though severely damaged by recent ISIS decimation)

By contrast, Damascus was all busy and bustle, but it was notably clean, and everyone was friendly and eager to be of assistance. This helped us find the required visa office, but on arrival we were told we had completed all the necessary formalities. We were lost so decided to ask an immaculately uniformed, traffic-directing, white-gloved policeman, complete with keffiyeh, for directions. We were hand-signalling but he couldn't respond as he was on a rostrum directing with energetic semaphore-like waving of his arms. So, to our utter astonishment, he said, in English, 'Go straight on, then take the first left followed by the first right'! We were so stunned we thanked him and nearly forgot his directions!

We passed through Deraa where Lawrence was tortured and interrogated by the Turks, and it was just as muddy and run down as portrayed in the film *Lawrence of Arabia*. Having read in a local brochure that the theatre at Bosra was the best in Syria if not the Middle East, we somewhat sceptically made another detour. But our reservations were unfounded, and indeed the theatre was just as had been described: without question the biggest we had seen and indeed the largest Roman theatre of the Middle East, with a seating capacity for 15,000 people. When the restoration of some of the columns are finished on the highest tier, it would surely be almost as good as new.

Again, we doubled back to the Syrian/Jordanian Customs. We were always somewhat nervous when arriving at these frontiers as, although we had what we believed were the correct visas and paperwork, a lot of it was unfamiliar to the officials and, of course, they had their own rules in their own languages. However, at some of the more remote borders, signing in as 'Stirling Moss' didn't seem to cause a problem!

Bosra theatre, largest Roman theatre in the Middle East, with seating for up to 15,000

Bosra theatre

The attitudes and contrasts between Syria and Jordan were dramatic, starting with the Customs and then the people, who were most courteous and helpful. Of course, all permeating down from my fellow Sandhurst officer cadet, HRH King Hussein of the Hashemite Kingdom of Jordan.

The countryside too was very different, being wonderfully lush and green, and we enjoyed the almost forgotten sensation of straight tarmac roads. There was a more relaxed atmosphere in Jordan, and we much enjoyed our time there. We followed the road to our last Roman remains at Jerash, considered to be one of the best preserved sites of Roman architecture outside Italy. It was nicknamed the 'Pompeii of the East' and founded from 7500-5500 BC. It hosted great conquerors such as Alexander the Great and the Emperor Hadrian. A series of civilisations lived at Jerash, including the Greeks, Crusaders, the Romans and latterly the Arabs. Coinciding with our arrival, we were pleased to welcome the sun making a belated appearance, which added to our enjoyment.

We were lucky to meet four Bedouin guards, complete with their traditional curved daggers (called janbiyas) and rifles, mounted on their bedecked camels.

After Jerash, we continued on to the Jordanian capital Amman, intent on enquiring at the tourist office for any information on Petra, but as ever the office was shut.

Royal Guards

Jerash

Jerash

We decided to push on to Jerusalem to watch the Palm Sunday procession in spite of not knowing its route or timings. Jerusalem is one of the three holy cities of Islam, the others being Mecca and Medina in the coastal Hijaz region of Saudi Arabia. By the time we had finished supper it was dark, but with only an estimated hour's drive we looked forward to reaching the city soon.

It was not to be. We were bowling along down a sloping tarmac road when, for reasons unbeknown to me, I decided to stop. I got out of the car and saw that not thirty yards in front of us the road had disappeared! It had completely given way, and there was just a dark chasm instead of a road. We had been very lucky. No choice but to retrace our steps and search for another route. However, we suddenly saw a small track to the left and hoped it was a recommended diversion. It quickly became obvious that without four-wheel drive there wasn't a chance of getting through. The 'track' was a quagmire, not helped by recent heavy rain, and on more than one occasion a digging-out session seemed imminent. With Gordon using a torch and leading the car, like a red flag warning in front of vehicles in the early days of motoring, and low-ratio four-wheel drive, we eventually rejoined the main road further down the valley. As Gordon remarked, 'Well, we are in the land of miracles!'

This opposite end of the highway was completely blocked and the man in charge of the barrier was so astounded to see a vehicle arrive from the other direction that he raised it without hesitation! We did, though, encourage him to erect a similar barrier or warning at the Amman end of the road.

We were now well below sea level, so it was a long climb up to Jerusalem, where we parked in the large open courtyard of the Palestine Archaeological museum.

Chapter 6

SERENITY AND SCRUB

Holy Land and through Iraq

The Old City, Jerusalem

THE NEXT MORNING we were so pleased with our parking place that we left the car to visit the tourist office for local information and to buy our standard breakfast of bread and oranges. The museum itself was a real pleasure apart from the entrance fee, though admittedly it did include the Dead Sea Scrolls exhibition. These scraps of parchment were utterly absorbing. Initially written in Hebrew during the second century BC, they narrate the religious and political life of the times. They have great historical significance because they include the second oldest known surviving manuscripts of the original Hebrew Bible. The scrolls were discovered in clay jars in a series of limestone caves hidden in the cliffs bordering the Dead Sea by a Bedouin shepherd boy searching for a lost sheep.

Now furnished with the route and times of the Palm Sunday procession, we moved the Land Rover to a more strategic observation spot and set about a maintenance check of the vehicle, particularly as it had been rather breathless of late. In order to get a good backdrop of the Garden of Gethsemane and the Church of All Nations it was necessary to grab some pavement space very early on, and thus we roasted for nearly two hours in blazing sun before the procession arrived. It formed up at the ruins of the Crusader castle in Bethany and then ascended the eastern slope of the Mount of Olives with halts for prayers and scripture readings. It was undoubtedly an international and very colourful gathering. Boy scouts, girl guides, nuns, monks and pilgrims lined both sides of the route with many coming down the centre bearing very beautiful, ornate banners. Everyone was carrying a palm frond and singing 'Hosannah, Hosannah' in their respective languages. The procession took an hour to pass, as we noted Lebanese, Americans, Thais, French, Scots, English and Germans.

Palm Sunday, Jerusalem

Still on the religious site-seeing trail, we left down a very steep and sinuous route through the hills to Bethlehem, some fourteen miles away, to visit the Church of the Nativity. This is believed to be the oldest Christian church in the world and the birthplace of Christ. It took seven years to build and was commissioned in 326 by St Helena, the mother of Emperor Constantine. You have to stoop to pass through the Door of Humility, which is only approximately four feet high and two feet wide, with the original intention of preventing horses and carts entering the church. The Grotto of the Nativity lies beneath the choiristry, and a simple silver star set in marble marks the place of Christ's birth. The Grotto also has a small, plain but beautiful altar marking where the manger stood. The church had an amazing atmosphere of peace and serenity, and the experience was very moving. We were sorry to leave and decided to return in the morning when we hoped there would be fewer tourists.

Carpenter's shop

Church of All Nations, Jerusalem

Church of All Nations, Jerusalem

Door of Humility, Bethlehem

We then left the village and drove down the road through open countryside to camp for the night in the local shepherds' fields. We were concerned when, during supper, a man appeared out of the dusk with a shotgun under his arm. Not to worry – he was very kindly inviting us to his home. We joined him, his wife, father and wife's sister sitting on the cushion-bedecked floor drinking tea. It was surprising the conversation we achieved since we knew so little of each other's languages! There we were, in fields just down the road from Bethlehem, by a camp fire, with shepherds, sheep and a brilliant star-studded night sky. It was exactly the same some 2000 years ago and whenever I hear the carol 'While shepherds watched their flocks by night', it takes me straight back to that evening.

Early the next morning we were back in the Church of Nativity after an unusually cold night. We spent a while there and afterwards saw the four Christmas Bells, which are traditionally rung a total of 33 times to symbolise the number of years Jesus Christ was believed to have lived.

We returned up the road to Jerusalem to visit the Garden of Gethsemane with its ancient olive trees reputed to have been there since the time of Christ. Next to the Garden is the beautiful and serene Church of All Nations, which is built over the Rock of Agony where Christ is said to have prayed before his arrest. To reach the tomb of the Blessed Virgin Mary you descend a wide flight of stone stairs, collect a candle and then wait to enter the actual tomb, as there is only room for two or three people at a time either standing or kneeling. The atmosphere in these sacred sites in my experience was very serene and moving. We climbed the Mount of Olives, having found the Russian Church closed, to the aptly named, simplistic Chapel of the Ascension. From this summit we had an exceptional view of the crenellated walls of Jerusalem and the strikingly beautiful Golden Gate, which has been closed for centuries. It is the gate through which Christ rode in triumph on Palm Sunday. In the Kidron Valley below there are hundreds of scattered tombs, prominent among them being Absalom's pillar, the tombs of St James and of Zachariah and Josphat. Entering the old city, we followed the Via Dolorosa at the foot of which is the Church of St Anne, which stands on the traditional spot where Anne and Joachim, Mary's parents, are believed to have lived at the time of her birth. These precincts also housed the Pool of Bethesda.

Tomb of Zechariah

Tomb of Absalom

Before continuing up the Via Dolorosa ('the route of pain'), we crossed over to the sacred enclosure with the Dome of the Rock and the Al Asque Mosque on Mount Moriah.

The Dome of the Rock is the third most holy site of the Muslim religion after Mecca and Medina. It was built in 691 and is of great significance to those who believe that the Prophet Mohammed's journey to heaven started from the centre of the shrine. The mosque is a superb example of Islamic architecture. The site is called the Temple Mount by the Jews and the Noble Sanctuary by the Muslims. It is believed that Jesus preached here and that it is the site from where Mohammed left for heaven.

The Dome of the Rock. Central Islamic shrine of Al Asque Mosque, which is built over the Foundation Stone where it is believed God created the world and Adam

We continued up the Via Dolorosa and passed the fourteen marked Stations of the Cross to reach the holiest church in Christendom, the Church of the Holy Sepulchre. This church is built on the site of the crucifixion, burial and resurrection. Within the church itself, there are many tombs and small chapels, which include Calvary. Just inside the entrance the traditional Stone of the Anointing, where Christ's body was prepared for burial, as well as the Chapel of the Mocking, the Chapel of the Division of Raiment and the Chapel of the Apparition. Also in the church is the Chapel of St Helen, where Christ's cross was found abandoned in a water cistern.

The most moving part of this visit was to spend time viewing the Tomb of Christ. However, such belief and tranquillity was often interrupted by priests of all denominations forcefully advising you that 'their' site was the 'actual' scene of a particularly religious happening and not least demanding a donation. After a while, this blatant commercialism overpowered any religious atmosphere one might have, which then transformed into a certain scepticism, if not cynicism.

Throughout the city we were impressed with the cleanliness and upkeep of the streets, which included the very active bazaar quarter.

After visiting the Wailing Wall, we left the Old City and drove around the outer wall to the Church of St Peters in Gallicantu, which was the new Assumptionist church commemorating Peter's denial of Christ and his repentance. It is built over the site of the Palace of Caiaphas, where Jesus was taken on the night of his arrest. This chapel is very modern, and we were shown around by a Franciscan monk whose narrative was in French, as we were joined by a group of French tourists, thus rendering English speakers in the minority. The tour included the dungeons where St James and other Christians were imprisoned.

The Wailing Wall

After a visit to the Anglican Cathedral of St George to research the times of the Easter services and a visit to the Tomb of the Kings, we needed a rest from religious sites and set off for the Dead Sea. Bordered by Palestine, Jordan and Israel, this is the lowest point on the surface of planet Earth at 1412 feet below mean sea level. It has (or had) a depth of just under 1000 feet, and its saline content is nearly ten times that of the oceans. Its main tributary is the River Jordan. However, it is currently receding the rate of approximately three feet per annum and also sinkholes are appearing.

The Qumrum Caves, site of the Dead Sea Scrolls discovery

We camped on the north west coast close to the Qumrum Caves where the Dead Sea Scrolls were discovered. The atmosphere – literally – was unique, with an almost oppressive stillness surrounding the countryside, which proffered little vegetation even in shady areas. A pre-supper 'swim' (or more accurately, 'float') taught me not to go underwater, as to regain the surface upright required some effort. We subsequently heard that several people had drowned, as they had dived into the sea and been unable to surface quickly enough. Having learnt this lesson, we were better prepared for the morning dip. The sun was up with scarce a ripple on the surface of the sea, which was crystal-clear. It took a long wade to get out of one's depth, but then trying to stand was near impossible, as the buoyancy took over and you found yourself horizontal! When we left the water and dried in the sun we were almost white, being covered by a layer of salt.

Later, we drove up to the caves where the scrolls were discovered and the excavated village of the long-departed Essenes who wrote them. A few more kilometres down the road we came to the sweet water springs of El Fusrah, where we enjoyed a refreshing, non-saline bathe and an equally pleasant supper. Our camping spot seemed to be a meeting place for mosquitoes, flies, bugs and any other insect, resulting in very little sleep that night. This probably wasn't helped by the fact that nearby was a good spot for the locals to wash their flocks of sheep and camels (hence the bugs!).

Today, 25th March, strong winds replaced the sun, which didn't help our photographic efforts in the Dead Sea with waves rushing towards us. We did, however, manage a photo of my floating horizontally reading the much-travelled copy of *Autosport*. As it happens, I did send the magazine some photos of their readership in Egypt and Jordan, and without any expenses claim, but never got a response.

Another refreshing freshwater bathe and we headed for the River Jordan, venue of Christ's baptism, and then on to Jericho on the west bank of the river. The site is one of the oldest continuous settlements in the world – as far back as 9000 BC! It has the oldest protective stone walls (maybe not to a certain someone?) in the world. It was taken from the Phoenicians by the Jordanians, who in turn lost it to the Israelis in 1947. In ancient times it was a centre for hunting and agriculture.

From there we went to the ruins of the Umayyad Palace where, unfortunately, most the famed mosaics were covered up. Luckily, the one named The Tree of Human Cruelty wasn't, and it was spectacular, dominated with vibrant green and gold tiles. The mosaic floors of this bath complex are considered to be the most beautiful in the world.

Not all the walls of Jericho came tumbling down

Mount of Temptation, appropriately located in the bleak Judean desert

By now with a fierce gale blowing a haze of dust, scrub and mist, we parked for the night at the foot of the Mount of Temptation. Whilst waiting for the overnight rainfall to abate, we met an Australian girl who was hitchhiking around the Holy Land, but we weren't challenged with the temptations that were reputedly made to Christ by the Devil! After lunch we made the steep climb to the summit, passing through the Greek Orthodox Monastery which somehow clings to the cliff face. The views from the top were spectacular over the vista of the Jordan valley, Dead Sea and the mountains of Gilead and Moab. We then returned to Jerusalem to park in the lea of the Golden Gate.

We were up at 5.30 a.m. to be in time to join the Anglican devotional walk up the Via Dolorosa, which was interspersed with halts for Bible readings and prayer. After the procession, we were seemingly swallowed up in a crowd of international tourists and pilgrims, all with the common interest of the Easter celebrations, which engendered an overall conviviality regardless of race or creed. That morning, we returned to the Garden of St Anne, the Pool of Bethesda, Golgotha and finally the tranquillity of the Garden Tomb.

Continuing the religious spectacular, we joined another international group – all groups seemed to morph from one to the other – for a final visit to the Church of the Holy Sepulchre. I was somewhat taken aback when an American lady turned to me and asked, 'What do you do when you get in there anyway?' My reply of 'It depends on why you want to go in there in the first place,' curtailed any further conversation!

Via Dolorosa

بستان قبر السيد المسيح
THE GARDEN TOMB
JESUS BEARING HIS CROSS WENT FORTH
INTO A PLACE CALLED THE PLACE OF A
SKULL, WHICH IS CALLED IN THE
HEBREW GOLGOTHA
WHERE THEY CRUCIFIED HIM, TWO OTHER WITH HIM
ON EITHER SIDE ONE, JESUS IN THE MIDST (John 19.17-18)

Garden Tomb

Golgotha

Having visited the Tomb and placed a further candle, I was fortunate enough to witness the Franciscan ceremony of enacting Christ's crucifixion and burial. A very moving service; in spite of not being able to understand a word, the meaning was clear.

Another very early start on Easter Sunday for the Sunrise Service at the Garden Tomb, which was packed with people from all corners of the world. The service was conducted by a padre from London, and the exemplary singing was provided by the Blind Children's Schools of both Jerusalem and Bethlehem. This unique experience was marred by German tourists noisily pushing to the front, taking flash photographs – and we hadn't even got beach towels!

That afternoon, we (again) ascended to the top of the Mount of Olives, offering the best view yet of Jerusalem. The Church of Paternoster on the summit is unique in that it has the Lord's Prayer inscribed on tablets in 44 different languages, including Basque and Gaelic. Such a melange of languages seemed appropriate as, coming to the end of a memorable Easter in Jerusalem, we reflected on the welcome and enthusiasm of the Jordanians. By far they had been the friendliest people we had met on the journey. Indeed, sometimes it got a little irritating, as suddenly they would appear seemingly from nowhere with endless questions: 'How are you? Where do you come from? You like Jordan? Have you seen, etc., etc.? Are you a student? I am a student and I am studying medicine. What do you do in England? Are you married? Where do you go? Why do you go to Australia? You work in Australia? Your father not mind you going to Australia?' Endless kind enquiries with many salaams and handshakes. Postage stamps for the children and cigarettes for the adults.

For the first time in seven years I wasn't at the traditional Goodwood Easter Monday motor racing. Quite a contrast but no regrets, as I felt I was deriving much more knowledge and satisfaction from this amazing journey.

We were on the verge of departing south when two Australian girls (suddenly there were a lot about!) turned up, requesting a lift to Petra. So, four-up somewhat cramped, we had to make a diversion via Amman as another road had collapsed. Once through Amman, straight across the desert to Naan to arrive at the designated parking area.

The main valley, Petra, Jordan

Petra, or 'The Rose Red City' as immortalised in John William Burgon's poem, owes this name to the rich colour variety of red, pink and purple sandstone rock from which all the buildings and dwellings were carved. The city lies in great folds of mountains, opening up into the Valley of Moses where reputedly he struck a rock and water gushed out. There is only one way into this amazing site, one of the world's greatest, ranking with Machu Picchu and Angkor Wat. This is via the Siq, which is a narrow defile in between 300-ft-high cliffs. It is so narrow it can only be traversed either on foot or horseback, so it is no surprise that it wasn't 'discovered' until 1812 by the redoubtable Swiss John Burkhardt, again disguised as an Arab, notably the first European to visit the city since the Crusaders.

We left behind a group of hopeful Arab grooms, who were disappointed we wouldn't hire one of their horses as we preferred to walk. The Siq, after several twists and turns, eventually opens out into the valley, and right in front of you stands the Treasury, an ornate and very striking façade carved out from the red sandstone and going back into the cliff face. It measures 43 metres high and 30 metres wide and was carved as a tomb for one of the first Nabataean kings. Many believed the 'Treasury' was just that, as attested by many pockmarks in the rock from bullets fired by frustrated robbers. It was first established in the fourth century BC by the Nabataeans, who were a nomadic tribe of Arabs, originally from Northern Arabia and the Southern Levant, and the city remained hidden for many years. The Greeks attempted to take the city a century later but were unable to sustain living in such a desolate location.

The Siq is the only way into the valley of Petra, which is why it remained a secret civilisation for so long.

Inevitably, the Romans arrived and destroyed Petra and rebuilt it in the second century AD; but throughout, the 30,000 hectares of temples, tombs and dwellings survived, despite a major earthquake in 33AD. The Nabataeans derived their wealth from trading, as Petra was a crossroads of major trade routes between Egypt, Arabia, Syria and the East. Silk from China, spices from India and incense from Arabia were all key commodities. In time, Palmyra to the north superseded Petra as a trade centre. At its peak the settlement hosted some 20,000 inhabitants, many of them troglodytes living in caves hacked out of the rock. Apart from its stunning major buildings, the Nabataeans built an incredible complex of cisterns, channels and reservoirs to capture the seasonal rainfall, which could be surprisingly sudden and heavy, as we knew from experience!

Earthquake damage to these systems contributed to the Nabataeans' departure. From the Treasury the valley opens out to include a carved Roman theatre with 33 rows of tiered seating for 3000 people, the Royal tombs, and the Urn, whilst all round and up the cliff faces are multiple houses and caves. At the end of the valley, after a stiff climb up some 900 steps, we reached the Monastery of El Deir, some 1000 metres above sea level. A panoramic view over the upper Rift Valley, down to Aqaba in the south and the Dead Sea to the north.

We eventually returned to Amman at 11.00 p.m. after a really stimulating and rewarding day. How much there is to see and learn, but you have got to go out and 'get it'. Fuelled with quince sandwiches and renditions of 'Waltzing Matilda', we learned a lot of useful and encouraging details of our intended destination, Australia, from our female hitchhikers. As their hotel was full we dropped them off at an accommodating police station, topped up with petrol and left the city to call a halt shortly after midnight. Thirty years later, one of the girls, Meg, traced Gordon via his uncle in Wagga Wagga and they met in Melbourne for dinner.

The Treasury

Petra: Tombs and theatre

Lower Valley with houses and cave dwellings

Ad Deir: 'The Monastery'

Cteisphon, Baghdad

We were up early after our late night, but not as early as we intended, and headed due east. The route was long and monotonous initially, through scorched, split rocks giving the impression of an extinct volcano. The Jordanian Customs were as efficient and courteous as before, and then we were into real desert, with the road running like a black scar through endless sand. There was little to see as the stark sandy landscape was bleak, to say the least, with the shimmering heat and constant mirages. Wandering Arabs with flocks of sheep and herds of camels would suddenly appear as if from nowhere but then gradually disappeared as we pressed on and came to the Iraqi frontier and Customs. With a fantastic sunset then darkness, like the switch of a light, we crossed the Euphrates to eventually park after just under 500 miles and a solid twelve hours' motoring. We got the impression that the firmament of crystal-clear myriad of stars and planets was smirking at our efforts whilst we camped in the sand near this historic river.

Washing and shaving obviously were not high on the Iraqis' agenda as a small crowd gathered the next morning to witness our ablutions. We then joined the endless queue of lorries and cars into the centre of Baghdad. Having eventually found the American Express office for our censored mail, we left the chaos of the city and made a short detour south of 20 miles down the Tigris river to Ctesiphon in Mesopotamia. The atmosphere in Baghdad was very tense, with many armoured cars bristling with machine guns. Whilst enjoying a brief coffee we fell into conversation with a resident, who told us that there had been six revolutions in the previous three years!

Ctesiphon was built on the original east bank of the Tigris in 58 BC, becoming the royal capital of the Persian Empire in the Parthian era for over 800 years. It was twice the size of Rome. During the endless Roman–Parthian wars it fell no less than three times to the Romans. It was also the site in World War I where the British and Indian army advance from Mesopotamia was halted by the Turks. During the sixth and seventh centuries it was one of the largest cities in the world. To this day, the Arch of Ctesiphon still stands and is the largest free-standing inverted arch in the world, built in the third century AD. The arch is a perfect parabolic curve so the bricks are in tension, resulting in it still standing whilst the rest of the building has almost disintegrated. The builders couldn't have been sure of the curve towards the base, as the walls are so very thick!

Compare Land Rover to size of arch

The largest free standing inverted arch in the world

The Hanging (no longer) Gardens of Babylon

Back through Baghdad and on to the Euphrates route, heading some 400 miles south to Basra. Having visited so many stunningly historic sites, we did not dwell long at a previous 'seventh wonder of the world', namely the Hanging Gardens of Babylon. Indeed, there seemed little interest from the authorities to restore, let alone maintain, it.

The illusory promising road, once we had cleared Baghdad, soon reverted to a dirt track once again. Before long we and the car were enveloped by choking dust allied to scorching heat, so we stopped at a local café for some water. This was equally full of dirt and dust so was quickly replaced by Coca Cola. We sat and watched the world go by: donkeys braying, lorries puffing, Arabs smoking hashish and spitting, dogs on the verge of starvation diligently searching for scraps, all accompanied by Winifred Atwell's honkytonk piano belting it out on the café's loudspeaker system. We pushed on to a quieter spot for the night and as we were about to clear up our supper, Gordon told me not to move, as trotting around at my feet was a scorpion. Apparently the smaller they are the more deadly they are, like this one, so we quickly replaced our sandals with desert boots.

The next day was again scorching, with the fierce sun bouncing back off the desert dunes with reflected heat. Except in a southerly direction (aided by our R.A.A.F. compass), the route of the rough potholed track, with its many diversions, was confusing, until eventually it petered out altogether. We were totally alone in a sea of sand, and eerily without an Arab, sheep, bird or camel to be seen. One had to keep one's nerve and not lose faith in a compass bearing or our own resolve.

More diverse track alternatives appeared, but then, like the promise of an oasis to liquid-craving travellers, we saw a line of telegraph poles in the distance. Easy, we thought: just follow them and we will find habitation! Then they disappeared behind a moving cloud of sand, to then reappear. We passed corpses of camels, endorsing no one is infallible in these harsh, unforgiving conditions. Without four-wheel drive we'd still be there, but eventually the poles changed to markers, which was encouraging. And then tarmac! However, it was so badly potholed we diverted back to the sand and four-wheel drive.

At last, Basra: Iraq's second city and only port, in spite of not having deep water access, but a major dock complex courtesy of British engineering and expertise. We headed straight for the police station to register as instructed by the frontier officials but were then told it wasn't necessary. Then the usual search for the American Express office. By the time we found it in a back alley, we knew the city of Basra intimately. Naturally it was shut, but after a long wait we collected our mail which, to our relief, included confirmation of insurance for Pakistan and India. Basra was known as 'The Venice of the East', as presumably the network of open sewers were considered sufficient to qualify for such a title with comparison to the famous Italian city. Latterly at an Australian cocktail party, Gordon met the Basra-based Australian Trade Commissioner's wife who, pulling no punches, told him that Basra was the arsehole of the Gulf and her husband was a shit for taking her there!

With not a lot to keep us in Iraq, not least being followed by a group of angry men waving fists and shouting insults so that we had to make a run for it, we were keen to get into Iran before the inevitable 'shut-down' of a Friday the following day. The so-called authorities, in their bureaucratic, chaotic wisdom, couldn't decide whether we should cross the Euphrates by ferry or by bridge, which resulted in us shuttling between the two as we tried to hide our frustration. Getting excited with the officials would certainly be counterproductive. Finally, we took the ferry in the early evening and got through the Iraq frontier formalities. It was then some 25 miles to the Iran Customs, which we were lucky to find, having followed another car across rutted, unsigned dirt tracks. The nondescript little official flexed his muscles, lit another cigarette, sucked his pencil and started to fill in countless forms. He then told us we couldn't retrieve our passports until the following morning. No way were we going to be parted from our most vital documents, so after a somewhat heated discussion we all proceeded to the nearby town of Khorramshahr, where a colleague completed all the formalities and stamped our passports. We thought we were free, but nothing is easy, as we were then instructed to safeguard a sheaf of these forms, a clutch of our Baker Street tube station photos and an identity card and to assure them we would report to a police station in every city we visited. A hot, hot day took us through to 11.00 p.m., and no amount of persuading from the police could make us move from our camping spot outside the town.

Chapter 7

TOUGH GOING

Basra to Quetta

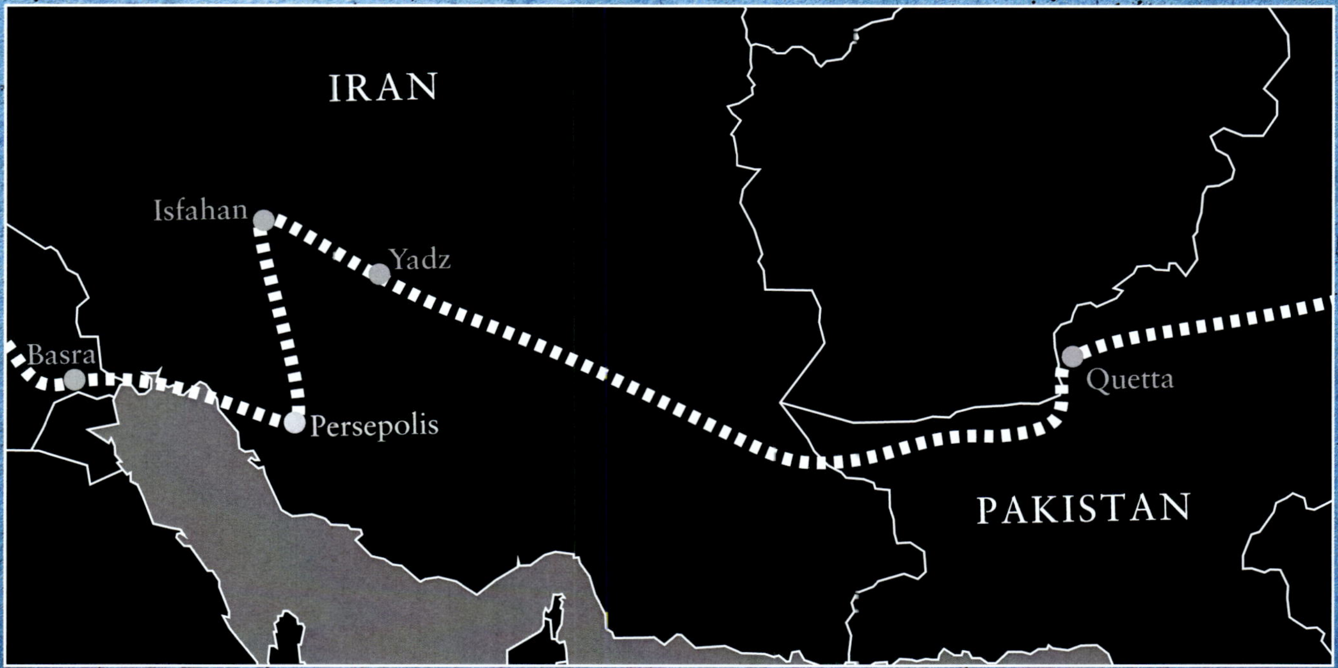

I DIDN'T HOLD any regrets on leaving Iraq which had an overall atmosphere of dirt, poverty, sad resentment and resigned apathy. The entire crossing of the country was through uninspiring scrub and sand not at all like the rolling sandscape of golden sands as portrayed in David Lean's stunning film *Lawrence of Arabia*.

Ctesiphon was the only scarcely appreciated and certainly not maintained worthwhile archaeological site, so we were looking forward to Iran with its dramatic mountainous countryside, famous blue tiled mosques and architecture.

You would be forgiven for thinking finding a petrol station in the town of Abadan – the regional capital, which boasted one of the world's largest oil refineries – would be easy, but this certainly was not the case. Eventually we did find one and topped up with fuel at only 2/4d a gallon, water, oil and battery levels. Then we set off to Shiraz, where we were directed on to what we believed was the correct road but then spotted traffic whizzing along dirt roads to our left and to our right! An oil pipeline obstructed getting to the left-hand route, so I diverted across what appeared to be a nice flat, hard strip to join the right hand lane of traffic. Big mistake: within thirty yards we had broken through the dry, cracked surface and descended into mud that had the gripping power of Loctite.

The Land Rover had sunk in so deep and so suddenly that both axles and some of the chassis were entrenched in a mixture of cloying mud and sand so we were lucky that we could even open the doors. We settled down to a long hot digging session which progressed to one of those memorable experiences which brings out the best in humanity.

A misconstrued 'short cut' arrival...

... several hours later, departure

After a couple of hours some locals arrived with their Jeep and tried to tow us out. No go, other than a broken tow rope! So a passing lorry was stopped, and we were engulfed by about thirty Iranians yelling different ideas and instructions as to how to extract these 'stupid foreigners' from the mud. This they eventually achieved by a combination of towing on sand mats, digging and communal shoving, all undertaken extremely cheerfully and seemingly thoroughly enjoying the distraction. After many salaams, handshakes, thanks and Rothmans were handed out, we set about cleaning ourselves and the car.

Forever climbing through the foothills of Iran

Apart from the slight modification of a nearby bridge we eventually reached our intended route. It was worth all the effort as it was the right road and in spite of dust storms reducing visibility to almost nil we pressed on through Bundar, Shapur and Oumidayen before starting a long sinuous climb through the foothills. At the first plateau we reached we halted for the night and were entertained by an array of large crude oil flames on the horizon – from the oil fields of Abadan – impressive against the night sky. The police visited us and told us to move on as the area was unsafe with thieves about. We declined but they returned, so this time we had no choice but to move further up the road. We left next morning in the early hours and our route was becoming forever steeper, crossing a series of mountainous ridges with beautiful plains in between. We often passed whole caravans of camels with all the attendant family's tents and belongings strapped to them.

We really felt we were going back in time as we were now on part of the ancient Silk Road, which for centuries linked China with Eurasia. Before we reached Shiraz, the dirt road became very steep and narrow, with a sheer cliff on one side and a long drop on the other. We couldn't afford to admire the dramatic views for too long as there was a steady stream of brightly painted, panting, grinding lorries and buses travelling in both directions. Sometimes it was like playing Russian roulette having to give way to a larger oncoming vehicle, as there weren't many places with only room for one to pass. Within 24 hours we had gone on dirt roads from the oil laden atmosphere of Abadan to the crisp mountain air of Shiraz at just under 5000 feet. Naive, law-abiding tourists that we were, we went to the police station to check in, as commanded at the border, but were told to return at the end of the day, to be then instructed to return the following morning. We filled in the time by visiting the local mosques and a bazaar displaying a huge array of lovely traditional carpets which frustratingly we couldn't consider through minimum finance and even less storage space.

Third time lucky next morning, as we were able to complete the required police formalities. The previous two days with our 'mud excursion' and constant dust storms had rendered the car like the interior of a flour mill, so a quiet spot was found and we set about cleaning it throughout and then ourselves.

With us and the car totally refreshed we set out for Persepolis, the site of one of the most ancient civilisations of the world. It was founded in 518 BC by King Darius and its name comes from the Greek meaning 'City of Persia'. It was sacked by Alexander the Great, reputedly requiring 3000 camels to transport the hoard of stolen treasures. It was built mainly on terraces to avoid the annual flooding of the Pulmar River and subsequent wet and marshy ground. The largest terrace covered some 125,000 square feet! Leading up to the Great Hall was a grand staircase sufficient in width to accommodate two horses side by side. This ensured that only those of noble birth could ascend without putting their feet on the ground trodden by lesser mortals. The sides of the staircase were adorned with bas-reliefs depicting the horses, chariots and attendant guards of the 23 subject nations. Of the Audience Hall or Apadana, only 13 of the original 72 columns remain. This hall, measuring over 2,000 foot square, could accommodate over 10,000 people. As it happened, Alexander must have hosted one of the most drunken victory celebration parties of all time. A lady challenged him to throw a burning torch into the palace, which quickly encouraged the many courtiers present to do the same and, as a result, aided by its many cedar wood furnishings, it was burnt to the ground! Quite a party! Some 200 years later the city was restored, improved and uprated by King Xerxes and his grandson Artaxerxes. Thus it basically remains as a melancholy ruin with a jumble of fallen columns, statues and archaeological debris. A truly memorable site to lost riches and splendours of the past.

Persepolis

Lion Capital

Reliefs at Persepolis

The loneliness of the long-distance Land Rover

Back in the real world, we pushed on some 300 miles to Isfahan, which is 200 miles south of Tehran, the capital of Persia/Iran since the 16th century. We had an unusual treat as our road was tarmac, so we made excellent progress across endless flat, uncultivated plains, flanked by snow-capped mountains in the far distance. We arrived in the late afternoon but turned in early after a very long day and with Gordon feeling pretty rough.

Shah Square, Isfahan

Isfahan is famous for its Persian/Islamic architecture, not least its magnificent mosques, palaces and covered bridges. The mosques rightly claim to be some of the most impressively decorated in the world, incorporating tiling instead of mosaics. The predominant colour throughout the mosques and buildings is a deep lustrous turquoise, the colour of ancient Persia. The Persian word for this colour also means 'water', most appropriately in such a parched country.

Shah Square, Isfahan

The ornately towered mosques are dominated by the turquoise tile, the colour of ancient Persia, representing water

Our search for the Post Office had its unforeseen rewards, passing along wide tree-lined boulevards not unlike Paris or Lisbon. These streets were immaculate with no sign of litter, and at each end there was usually a fountain or roundabout. Its main square, Shah Square, is one of the largest in the world and was surrounded by ornate, fountain fronted mosques, with their constant loud speaker entreaties of the Iman calling for prayers. All very impressive, with an almost overpowering command of respect of the Islamic religion. It was built from 1598 to 1629 and is now a UNESCO World Heritage listed site.

We left Isfahan, this time on our more familiar dirt road, following the incorrect directions to Yazd. This road was particularly bad, and indeed the term 'road' was a generous one. Just as it was becoming almost impassable, we came to a large junction of tracks without one signpost between them. We flagged down a lone lorry and after much flapping of arms, head-scratching and sign language, the driver confirmed we were on the wrong road and so we returned to Isfahan, where the whole enquiry process started again. After many such enquiries we set off, although I must admit somewhat sceptically as this road wasn't much better than the first. However, we pushed on, covered in clouds of dust both outside and through every crack and crevice of our long-suffering Land Rover. Strong winds added to the discomfort and reduced visibility.

We were all the time climbing and, just before Nairn, crested a pass of 7000 ft. This was a very bleak landscape indeed, and not totally confident of our exact position and the potential of a fuel station in spite of topping everything up in Isfahan, we were somewhat nervous of running out of petrol. Such was the terrain we suffered another tyre star fracture. This necessitates levering off the entire tyre, comprehensively patching it, reattaching it onto the wheel and inflating with the foot pump. Not to be recommended in windy, hot, dusty conditions! These tyre star fractures were mainly caused by the abject condition of the road surface and were cause for concern, quite apart from the hassle of repair, as depending on how close the fractures are they can render a tyre totally useless as it loses all its rigidity.

We reached Yazd (meaning God) at dusk. This was once a cross roads of the great trade routes from China and India and is the last stronghold of Zorastrianism, which is the worship of fire. The main temple hosts a constantly burning flame and has some 10,000 followers. During the rampant invasion of Genghis Khan, Yazd became a sanctuary for many artists and intellectuals fleeing his invasion of Persia. Thus we decided to call a halt outside the town to cook our dinner on our own dedicated fire.

The next morning neither of us felt very enthusiastic about anything, myself after a gigantic nosebleed and Gordon with the aftermath of what we assumed was 'flu. It was the same story of very rough roads and endless dust. Without such debilities we would have spent some time exploring the town but decided to press on. There was nothing attractive in these intimidating surroundings and the drive almost became a challenge as opposed to enjoyment.

The landscape was bleak, dry, barren and a confused jumble of crumbling, black rock formations, rubble and swirling, penetrating dust. We both looked like old men, with grey dust-coloured hair and eyebrows, and it didn't make much difference if you washed it off as it soon returned. Two hundred miles further on, the scenery improved and we were flanked again by another series of snow-capped mountain ranges which seemed to be laughing at our puny efforts.

The aforementioned tyre star fractures hit us again with a vengeance, with five in one tyre rendering it useless. A good thing we had bought another in Madrid which we were able to inflate with the help of a passing lorry driver's compressor.

Tough going; the compass vital in the ever-shifting- wind-blown sands

Not surprisingly, two young foreigners attracted a lot of curiosity, but with a few notable exceptions the overall atmosphere was of friendliness and helpfulness, especially if one was out on the road. We were lucky to meet this driver as our own air pump, in spite of continual re-builds, had had it!

We chugged on for another 360 miles through this seemingly never-ending dumping ground of all the rubble and rock that had been surplus to building the world, crossing several dried-up river beds which a few weeks earlier in the season of melting snows would have, without question, halted our progress. This was not a factor we had considered in our route planning, but having said this such information would have been hard to come by.

The following morning the featureless landscape improved to a modicum of fertility which quickly disappeared, giving way to desert. We crossed interminable expanses of shingle and sand which was never still owing to the encouragement of continually strong winds. Towards the end of this stretch we crossed a few wadis, but in the main we required the assistance of four-wheel drive.

We arrived at the foot of an Afghan pass and surmised we might have to go right down to the very lowest churning ratio of the gearbox as our route went up the entire length of a dried-up riverbed. Slow progress was made through dramatic, brooding mountain ridges in ever-changing hues of purple and green, adding to the intimidating atmosphere. We crested the pass only to be confronted a few miles later by another one before the remaining few miles into Zahedan.

Fortune smiled upon us on arrival in the town where we met what some would call an 'opportunist' or 'businessman', whilst others would call him a 'spiv'! Notwithstanding, he was happy to change money so we could fill both our fuel tanks to the brim together with two separate cans which we could hide in the car, as the Pakistanis would not allow the import of fuel to ensure you bought their own very expensive petrol. We then repaired to an hotel room where negotiations took place with our entrepreneurial friend to part-exchange seven new wrist watches for our table and chairs and five-gallon water carrier. We then hid this valuable 'currency' in with our shampoo and toothpaste supplies and thus felt we were well equipped for the rumoured expense of Pakistan.

When we emerged from the hotel there was a ring of people surrounding an unfortunate man writhing on the ground. He was screaming, spitting, flapping and tearing at his clothes whilst thrashing his arms to the jeers, derision and torments of the many onlookers. A rabies victim undoubtedly, but there was nothing we could do except hope his sufferings would end sooner rather than later. A very disconcerting sight.

Shortly after leaving Zahedan, there was a loud 'crack' from the rear of the car and we discovered that a main leaf of the rear spring had broken. Hardly surprising after the battering of the last three days' motoring, but the nearest Land Rover agent was in Lahore, some 1200 miles distant. Nothing for it but to keep going at a mere 30 mph, which is not recommended over continual cross-corrugated roads. Ideally on such roads, to minimise a vehicle being battered to bits and your teeth falling out you need to travel either at 10 mph by driving slowly over the continual ruts or at a minimum 65 mph so you skim them. Both out of the question for us, given our broken spring.

We passed through the Iranian Customs, leaving them a 'Stirling Moss' signature as the driver and into Pakistan. The change was dramatic and although the road was still dirt, there were signposts and whitewashed marker boulders which were much appreciated, especially at night! With Gordon not feeling at all good again we set up camp in a sort of 'No Man's Land' between the Pakistan frontier and their Customs post. The next morning on arrival at the Customs, we were admonished for stopping where we did as we had camped in a notorious bandit area, but luckily again we had seemingly not been worth bothering about. All the while now, owing to the damaged spring, we had to keep our speed very low but sometimes there were stretches of tarmac. Of much more concern though was Gordon's fever which appeared to be getting worse not better. He was very weak, unable to stand from a squatting position, so he went to 'bed' in the back whilst I pressed on as fast as the springs and conditions would allow. We needed to get to Quetta and medical assistance as soon as possible and, to an extent, to hell with the concerns of the spring. The road now was almost obliterated by swirling sand and dust necessitating reliance on the use of our compass. Gordon was (in the back of the Land Rover) now in pain and delirious. We skirted a large salt lake and were now in the real desert with waves of wind flecked sand dunes marching to a shimmering horizon. Dust and sand covered the road. We and the car were not in good shape to make this crossing and the responsibility for Gordon's health was frightening, especially as I had no real idea of how long it would take to reach help. After nearly a hundred miles, thankfully, the desert was replaced by mountains and after crossing three passes and 320 miles of slow motoring eventually, to our relief, we reached the mountain town of Quetta, 5500 feet above sea level on the border of Afghanistan and the capital of Baluchistan, on the 9th April.

Quetta, the highest city in Pakistan, was famous for its fruit production and in the 19th century was a strategic centre for the flourishing British Empire. However, in 1933 it suffered a major earthquake, which killed an estimated 40,000 people. More importantly to us, it had a hospital where Gordon was promptly examined and then put straight to bed, whilst I went and parked on the outskirts of the town – thankful that he was under the watch of qualified medical staff.

Even though Gordon was now under proper medical care, it was obvious next morning that a permanent bed with constant supervised care was imperative. As was my wont I had yet again parked in a military area next to the hospital, which was enlivened by a Punjabi pipers and buglers school not calculated to improve Gordon's aching head. All the military hospital could do was to provide him with some strong knock-out pills – nothing new there, then! Thus for the time being, a bed in the tourist rest house was the quietest spot to be found for the day. Gordon was no better the following morning and I was becoming very worried about his condition and finding him proper medical care, but it took two days to do so by returning to the Mission hospital from the rest house. I explained the situation to a young English doctor, who promptly admitted

Gordon to a private room whilst I put my sleeping bag on the verandah. The senior doctor, Dr Holland, and his wife were most sympathetic, supportive and helpful.

Gordon was to undergo tests for typhoid and malaria, with a predicted stay of at least two weeks in the hospital. The local rules dictated that if you had a relative in hospital then the family were responsible for providing their meals. The Hollands obviously took the view that if such was left to me then Gordon's chances of survival would be severely diminished. Thus they kindly offered to look after him themselves, which was comforting and generous of them, to say the least. It was a huge relief to know at last he was in very good, caring, qualified hands.

Quetta was on the main hippy route from Europe, so during my time there I met many other travellers from all over the world: Australians stranded in their broken down bus; a German who had been on the road for over five years; two Americans who had driven up from Nairobi; and an English brigadier who obviously believed the Raj way of life still existed. Being fluent in Urdu, the local language, he had the Punjabis busy cleaning his Triumph 2000, doing his washing and cleaning his clothes! He claimed to be a friend and frequent guest of President Nehru of India, and I learnt a great deal from him about the Indian way of life, with his colourful predictions for the country's future having only obtained its Independence from Britain some 16 years earlier.

The large noticeboard at the Pakistan frontier which said 'Welcome to Pakistan, Land of Hospitality' was regarded by some with great scepticism, but for us, and especially myself now on my own so to speak, it certainly rang true. Often such approaches had an ulterior motive, such as an English address or better still an English reference, which could be used to further a visa or passport application. I spent many hours in Quetta drinking innumerable cups of tea, which is the traditional welcome. I made the acquaintance of a baker of pitta bread; a tailor who repaired my anorak; a mechanic who made minimal charge for fabricating a new leaf for our broken spring and most importantly, a restaurateur. The repair was achieved with the assistance of an interpreter who liaised with me and a group of 'mechanics', some little more than twelve years old.

The bazaars all had different small enclosures – or, to be absolutely frank, hovels – for the many different trades. I was somewhat dubious when I was advised that a blacksmith was the man was to repair the spring, but apparently such a title also covered his skills as a builder, painter, mechanic and odd job man. Whilst I squatted in their small hut drinking copious amounts of tea from oil smeared cups the 'blacksmith' and his many assistants set to work. In the neighbouring space the proprietor was busy heating brake lines in a large pot over a fire. Then he would remove one when duly hot and carefully scrape it until the copper shone brightly and put it to one side for purposes not mentioned. I could only presume they would then melt it down and sell it for its intrinsic value.

Local 'garage' Quetta, fabricating a new leaf spring

Chapter 8

WELCOME OR NOT?

Pakistan and India

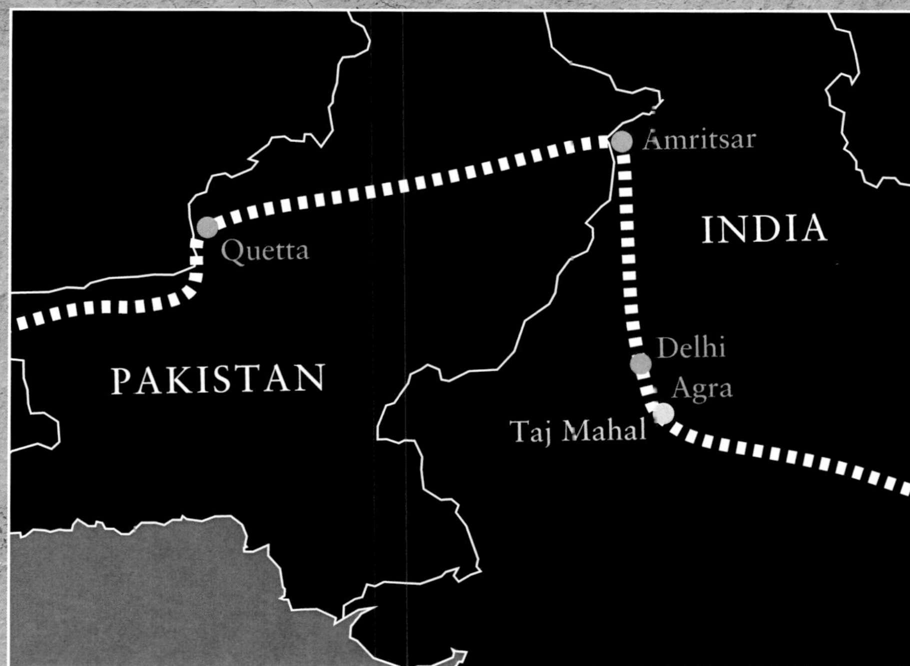

TWO DAYS LATER Gordon seemed much improved having undergone treatment for malaria, but he still had severe backache which Dr Holland attributed to lumbago. I was pleased however to be able to repay some of the hospital's help by going to retrieve their ambulance Land Rover, which had broken down some 25 miles west over the other side of the pass. I towed it back to find that the clutch had burnt out, and an urgent request was sent to Karachi for a new plate.

The Hollands kindly invited me to join them for supper, but then this invitation was trumped by some of the local dignitaries inviting us all to a traditional 'Surdu'. This is a local version of a barbecue, with long trenches filled with burning wood over which are roasted large chunks of sizzling mutton. Accompanying the meat were acres of salads, pitta bread, fruit and gallons of beer. A real feast to a nomad used to alcohol-free meals and packets of soup for the past few months. A fact endorsed by my return to the hospital verandah in the wee small hours whilst attempting a polka with an expectant mother! There was an interesting cross section of guests, from the medical staff to the local dignitaries, staff college members and Australians, Canadians, British and Americans. The latter were members of the American Peace Corps in their ubiquitous green Jeeps, who often seemed to be regarded with a high degree of resentment.

I also met a couple who had spent many months living with one of the local tribes whom they narrated were 'pretty primitive'. For instance, they didn't murder an enemy but would simply smash both legs for the longer pleasure of seeing the victim crippled for the rest of their life. Indeed, John Speke, the noted 19th-century African explorer, had used the very tough Baluchi tribesmen as his core bearers on his explorations of Somalia and Central Africa. This attitude was endorsed when I spent the morning in the company of a blind man who had been cruelly maimed rather than killed. One evening he had answered a knock on his door to have a bucketful of sulphuric acid thrown in his face. In spite of his appalling injuries and loss of sight he was extremely cheerful, and we had a rewarding discussion.

The Hunchback of Notre Dame in the local cinema and supper with two Canadians completed my day, but they were not encouraging about the Australians' condemnation of narrow-mindedness, arrogance and resentment of immigrants. We discovered later that there were two sides to that story and many of the British immigrants, who constantly referred to 'whatever the situation, it was always better back home'. Nine times out of ten the response was in two words – one of four letters and the other of three. We would no doubt find out for ourselves and form our own opinions.

Gordon's fever had all but gone, but his back condition and attendant pain, if anything, were becoming worse. The doctors couldn't identify the cause and we were all getting frustrated with no real diagnosis which, above all, was the priority and once known perhaps we could continue with our journey? A lumbar puncture was taken, but since the pathologists were on leave no diagnosis could be achieved. Nothing could be progressed in the short term, so I repaired to the Rest House where I caught up on the news with back copies of the *Observer* and *Newsweek*. One morning, as I was obviously British, I was cornered by an angry Pakistani who subjected me to a three-hour tirade concerning the politics of Pakistan, India and Kashmir – a very animated, narrow-minded debating agenda, fuelled by the aftermath that the Raj of British rule engendered. The suggestion that the countries had benefitted from the British investment and installation of the railway system, education and hospitals, etc., was scarce acknowledged, let alone appreciated. No love lost there, then!

No improvement again the next morning for poor Gordon who was in constant pain so my hospital guide, John Sandford-Smith, in the absence of the pathologists, attempted to define the spinal fluid from the lumbar puncture himself. He sadly was thwarted, announcing he couldn't tell the cells from the dust. He even asked *me* what I thought about the results! The initial medical concern seemed to have evaporated into lethargy, which was both very worrying and frustrating. Gordon now looked like an unemployed pastry chef with white smock, pantaloons and small dough cap. There was nothing more that could be done for the time being, and it was with sadness and reluctance that John and I drove to a nearby lake for an invigorating seven-mile walk under the watchful gaze of the brooding, intimidating mountains.

Dr Holland decided the next morning that a second opinion as to Gordon's condition was imperative. Great – but who, when? Again, nothing I could do. So following an exciting invitation from a pilot I met at the Surdu, I headed for the local aerodrome to go gliding. Take-off is dramatic, with a winch towing the glider to climb quickly and urgently almost vertically to release at 600 feet. Then we were slowly and silently floating over the cantonments and parade grounds of Quetta, followed by the vista of the harsh, rugged mountains, many of which had previously looked down on us as far as one could see.

A dramatic, striking and unforgiving landscape with a bloody, uncompromising history. I later met the Chief Instructor, who had set a personal flight record of 20,000 feet above sea level. His generous offer of doing some soaring later in the week did somewhat brighten the gloomy concerns of the moment.

It took a further three days wait before 'Mr Second Opinion' arrived to give Gordon a thorough examination, and at the end of the day we got the results. Apparently only severe back ache with a projected cure of exercise and stretching on what can only be described as a 'rack'! Not very convincing or encouraging. We were assured as a result of these 'cures' we would be back on the road in a few days but we were sceptical with this prognosis, to say the least.

That evening I joined Joseph, the maimed victim, and his family to show them our colour slides and describe our visit to the Holy Land and although, sadly he couldn't see them, they were much appreciated in spite of just having to rely on description!

Next day the 'unemployed baker' staggered out of the hospital to collapse onto a chair in the roasting sun. This and a 'rack' session scarce helped his condition. We were now by this point getting more than concerned as the best way forward in every sense as we had to consider either aborting the journey or continuing by myself. Above all, we had to know the cause and then hopefully in turn the cure of Gordon's illness and severe pain.

Glider

Another unexpected diversion was welcome, with an invitation to go hunting with a group of locals, so we set off to the now familiar Hannah Lake. Unfortunately, the chap with the promised hunting rifles and the guide failed to make the agreed rendezvous. Thus we had an excited group of Pakistanis with a motley collection of arms from a shotgun to a . 400 and a . 22, who blazed away indiscriminately at anything that to them seemed to move or, at worst, anything that did not. The ensuing scenario was even more hilarious in spite of not hitting a single victim with the hail of lead, but they certainly enjoyed themselves. Returning to the hospital later, I met a local garage owner who bizarrely assured me he had a recipe of crushed herbs that would cure Gordon but not my knee, since it had been previously operated on. A genuine offer but not one we took up as, not least, that wouldn't have endeared us to the hospital staff.

We had now spent just over two weeks in Quetta where everyone had been very helpful and supportive but, in every sense, we had to make a positive move. Gordon's health was the priority, but an accurate, reliable diagnosis and cure was obviously not forthcoming in the near future. He was now mobile with no fever but weak, so it was decided to push onto either a major hospital and if a diagnosis was achieved to then consider the possible completion of the journey to Australia or a return to UK for treatment. This decision was reinforced now by the company of a Dutchman, Carel, whom I had met in Quetta and would take the place of Gordon's driving or other demands had continuation of the journey remained with just the two of us.

We were ready to leave, and I had whittled down my belongings to just a rucksack in case I was to continue by myself. At this point the hospital announced they wanted to take another blood test and we should delay until the results were known. However, we decided that if such tests did show anything they could be forwarded to a hospital in Delhi, together with the bill for all the medical costs. We enjoyed a final dinner with the ever-generous Robsons, who had been very supportive and hospitable throughout our stay, before an early start the following morning. Spirits were high and so was the sun as we left after nearly three weeks in Quetta.

The first hundred miles proved uneventful, and we crossed the Bolan Pass to follow the twists and turns of an adjacent watercourse. I took over after Gordon had valiantly but probably foolishly insisted on contributing to the driving but we had to stop several times for him to be sick. It was viciously hot, with the melting tarmac (seemingly) throwing up more heat. We were in a mobile oven and skin contact with the Land Rover's bodywork resulted in a nasty burn.

A few miles before Surkur we heard the depressing hiss of another flat tyre. Carel and I got out and, with sweat pouring off us, proceeded to change the wheel whilst Gordon hung out of the passenger window liberally fertilising the ground below! In a very short space of time there was a roaring in my head and my vision blurred only to blackout with obvious sunstroke. I hazily came to, to find a group of Pakistanis had come to our aid and were changing the wheel for us. We were all in bad shape so early that afternoon, after the fourth attempt, we found a rest house in Surkur whose only vacant bed was allocated to Gordon. Carel and I went to the local railway station for some sustenance and after a 70-minute wait the wrong order arrived. We still had a tyre problem to sort out, but with the aid of cigarettes and a dodgy air line we achieved this before collapsing onto our sleeping bags where we slept for twelve hours straight.

Back to the railway station for a late 'breakfast' the next morning as we had been told that the most reliable restaurants were at the stations, which had been established by the British when building the rail networks throughout Pakistan and India. The previous day's temperature had apparently been 115°F in the shade, which no doubt accounted for my sunstroke. Today wasn't any cooler.

We crossed the wide, turgid Indus river, with the water the colour and consistency of chocolate blancmange. The road was crammed with lorries, buses, bullock carts and pony traps, and we often had to lurch off it to avoid oncoming vehicles. One gentleman refused to look before crossing the road and despite horn-blowing and our taking violent avoiding action, our nearside mirror neatly took the axe he was carrying out of his hand. It didn't do our mirror any good, but I think he might consider looking before crossing again in future. We crossed the Indus three more times before we reached Multan, where we managed to find a three-bedded room in the rest house to occupy with the promise of vacating by 7.00 a.m. the next morning.

The decision to stop overnight at rest houses and eat at the railway stations was justified. After all, there wasn't room for three of us to sleep in the Land Rover and it was an oven even at night. Further and very importantly, it gave the brave Gordon, who was far from fit, a chance to get a better night's rest and have immediate facilities if required. The food at the stations was of a higher standard and choice than we could have prepared ourselves and, again, we were not equipped for three. More room, more choice, better conditions and good value. One of the many standards instigated by the British, and inherited and perpetuated by the locals.

We were up promptly and after a short argument regarding the doubling of the quoted bill, we set off to Lahore, some 220 miles distant. A muddled combination of tarmac and dirt roads and an even bigger challenge getting through Lahore itself, but Cairo traffic still got the prize, owing to the faster speed of the vehicles and the ratio of cars to animals. We stopped at a restaurant and were sitting outside when a flock of sheep were driven though the tables. On the other side there was the bloated dead body of a camel which judging by the smell had obviously been there for quite some time. In Australia I was asked by a Pakistani taxi driver what I remembered about Lahore and I replied, 'The wildlife!' There was no reason to linger in the city, and we soon reached the frontier some 18 miles further on. Prior to India's independence in 1948, this border was decided by lawyer Sir John Radcliffe with the objective of trying to separate the respective Muslim religious majority of Pakistan from the Hindu followers of India.

River Indus

We were confronted by three separate checkpoint buildings with approximately 200 yards between them both on the Pakistan side and then on the Indian side with the border in between. Apart from a long wait, we got through the three Pakistani checks without a problem, but at the first Indian checkpoint we hit trouble. Contrary to his belief, Carel was unable to obtain a visa at the frontier, which meant a visit to Karachi some 800 miles behind us to get one. In spite of every persuasive argument we could muster, except very risky bribery, it was useless. So we took Carel back to the Land Rover under the pretence of getting his belongings out and promptly buried him under rucksacks, biscuit tins, blankets and anything else to hand. We told him, on pain of imprisonment for all of us, not to move under any circumstances or make a sound. As a concession he was allowed to breathe! We then drove up to the second Indian building which housed the Customs, but luck deserted us there as the formalities took nearly an hour. The Customs then wanted to check the engine number against the carnet but I managed to dissuade them. There now remained one more building to clear and, after a whispered apology to Carel, who was, in every sense, slowly melting under all our baggage, we told him under no circumstances could he move. Then we hit another problem: the officials were very concerned my passport had a South African stamp in it, as India contributed to the boycotting of the country in retaliation to its apartheid policy. After much banter and convincing them that I had only been on a brief holiday, they let us through into India. We hurtled around the next few corners and pulled up by some bushes to extract Carel from his sweatbox in the back of the car.

It was absolutely baking hot, with a constant shimmering heat haze off every surface and Carel was very dehydrated, but this was easily countered by his relief of getting through into India, further aided with copious gulps of tepid water. Fine, but we wondered what problems he would face trying one day to get out of the country. Months later, a postcard arrived informing us that he was back in Holland and had managed to make his exit from India on the promise of returning with an accommodating white girl!

India immediately was apparent with its colourful vibrancy – the women in beautiful shimmering saris and many of the men in brightly coloured turbans. Amritsar, in the state of the Punjab, is the centre of the Sikh religion and like so many of the cities we visited has a bloody history, not least after a massacre by British troops of at least 400 peaceful protesters demanding self-government in 1919. The Golden Temple is the focal point of the Sikh religion and has been the scene of many riots and demonstrations.

We commenced on a rigorous search for Major Puri, the Indian surgeon who had been recommended to me by the Brigadier 'Raj' in Quetta. During the course of our enquiries we met a very hospitable Sikh, who insisted he entertain us at his home with tea and mangoes. On being introduced to his wife, we made the mistake of shaking her hand. When she happened to leave the room, her husband told us that this was unacceptable in their society but acknowledged it was an innocent mistake. During this generous hospitality we learnt a lot about the Sikhs and their history, when one of the guests advised us that Major Puri lived some 150 miles up the road!

We were back on the road the next morning bright and early to try and avoid the stifling heat of the day. Now we were on much better tarmac, often bordered by shady trees which helped to minimise the glare of the sun. Having said this, the driving standards were at best unpredictable and at worst chaotic, so one had to be constantly on the watch for unscheduled manoeuvres and sudden illogical changes of direction. We had in the course of meeting other travellers been given two major warnings about driving in India. Firstly, cows in India are considered sacred and in all circumstances have right of way, so do not hit one, let alone kill one, otherwise you could be swiftly arrested. Secondly, be very careful in the more remote areas, where 'granny', already dead some time, might be thrown under your wheels with the entire village then 'in witness' pointing accusations of lethal driving, with the only solution to the 'crime' being compensation.

On arrival at Ambula, we were told that the famed Major Puri was based in the nearby military hospital and thus we ran him to earth in the operating theatre. It was a huge relief to meet him, and he was immediately most welcoming and helpful. He and a fellow surgeon quickly set about examining Gordon and took several samples and X-rays.

Unlike previous tests, the results came through quickly. We were advised Gordon had stones in his kidneys resulting from a urinary infection, which not least explained the constant debilitating pain. Major Puri assured us it was quite in order for Gordon to continue if we didn't do too much driving or overdid things. Our frustration at having, to a degree, spent so much time in Quetta was superseded by relief that Gordon's illness wasn't more serious and not least we now knew what we were dealing with. The Major's recommended cure was 'eight pints of beer a day' to flush out the stones, starting in the Officers Mess that evening. That prescription and being armed with a pain-killing 'bomb' were apparently all we needed to complete our journey provided Gordon didn't overdo things. Thus within an afternoon we were all set to continue, now armed with boxes of pills and medicines. Whilst trying to check into a rest house, we were told the English were unwelcome, and it was the first of many oft-repeated, post-Independence resentments, often finishing with the phrase 'f*****g British bastards'! Coincidentally, Major Puri told us when he was an exchange doctor with the British army he had a like experience when seeking lodgings in London. He said there was a lot of similar resentment to Pakistanis and Indians in the UK at that time.

No problem, though, with the next rest house on this occasion. After supper, we gratefully accepted Major Puri's kind invitation to a beer (a practice flushing-out session?) in his front garden, followed by a visit to the nearby Officers Mess, where he told us many useful and interesting facts about India. His military colleagues were more British than their British officer counterparts, with their waxed moustaches, cravats and striped blazers drinking 'pinkers' – pink gins (gin and angostura bitters) – a favourite tipple of the Raj! And did they drink! As the consumption increased so did the tallness of their stories, until we had double-headed cobras racing the horses on the Calcutta racetrack. But the prize went to Major Puri, who narrated how he was bivouacked somewhere on the North West Frontier and was summoned by the Subedar Major to deal with a tiger which was menacing the troops in their tents. In his own words, the Major started to narrate how everyone 'was very inebriated but we sent the ....' – sadly the solution, shall we say, was lost 'in the translation'! I couldn't remember much after that other than at some point we were all on 'all fours' pretending to be tigers chasing each other around a large Banyan tree! Unfortunately we didn't consume enough beer to flush out Gordon's kidney stones, but it wasn't for the want of trying.

A break in the normal traffic chaos

Delhi turned out to be a huge disappointment ,with many of its streets unkempt, run-down and dirty. It was quite a drive to get to Connaught Place, the centre, since one firstly had to battle through the traffic of the walled city of Old Delhi. You don't actually drive but as gently as possible force your way or simply get swept along through totally chaotic thoroughfares that are jammed with bullock carts, pony traps, buses, dogs, cats and endless humans, most of whom are shouting and yelling, and the ubiquitous tuk-tuks. The latter are basically three-wheeled, Vespa-engined scooters mounted by a death-wish driver carrying a maximum of two passengers behind him. They are a total nightmare, constantly diving for gaps that don't exist, so one had to be very firm and exercise the South American principle that the 'larger you are the more priority you have'! Obviously, I hadn't reached Delhi when I nominated Cairo as the most chaotic city to drive in!

We found the cheapest hotel available and after an excellent supper attempted to sleep 'on' the bed as opposed to 'in' it. Although the overhead fan was flat out the atmosphere was sweltering even in early May, and the hubbub of the streets below never ceased. Rather than batter our way next morning through the frenzied traffic, we risked everything and hailed a tuk-tuk, which brought out a few motor racing comparisons and memories of the dodgems at local funfairs.

Now we had the medical assurances for Gordon, we considered two possible penultimate destinations before Australia – either Kathmandu or Singapore. If it was the former, we would sell up the Land Rover and fly out, and if it was the latter, we would ship to Perth and drive across the Nullabor to 'Wogga'.

No problem re a visa for Nepal but as regards Malaya we were advised such only could be obtained in Calcutta (now Kolkata) just under a thousand miles away. Decision made for us, so we returned to the Land Rover and cruised the wider, fountain-ornate streets of the Parliament and Consulate area. However, here we got the distinct impression that it was a very exclusive area, only fit for members of Parliament and the Diplomatic Corps. That evening, since we were in the capital of India we had to try a local curry! Mistake! I have had better ones in South Kensington!

Carel at this point had decided to stay in India for several months, no doubt contemplating how he was going to get out of the country, and he took a bus to some remote village in the north. Gordon and I, however, set off in the opposite direction, some 120 miles south to Agra. Travelling in India on a Sunday resulted in a distinct lack of the usual honking, careering lorries and buses. All along our route huge flocks of sheep and herds of bullocks were wandering aimlessly around completely unattended. Great listless mounds of yellow corn lay awaiting the trampling and threshing that were due by the bullocks the next day. It would appear that the only activity of the day were the animals soaking themselves in lakes of stagnant water.

Taj Mahal, Agra

Outside the Taj Mahal

The Taj Mahal is considered one of the most beautiful buildings in the world and is by far India's most visited tourist attraction. It took some twenty-one years and 20,000 people to build it in the 17th century. A white tomb in memory of the Mughal Emperor's favourite wife, Mumtaz Mahal. Built entirely in white marble it has many fountains watering wide deep green lawns in front and behind flows the turgid Yamuna River. Perhaps we were a bit 'site-seeing blasé', but we were not that impressed with the Taj, with its constant begging and an open sewer behind the building. India presented a paradox: on the one hand huge wealth and on the other extreme poverty, with little chance of changing one's lot. The archaic 'caste system' more or less dictates your life from birth, and we felt as long as that existed the vast minority could not further themselves.

An early night and a self-cooked dinner, as surprisingly and unusually the train station didn't have a restaurant. The British-laid railway network is the key to travel in India with every available space inside the carriages, on top of them and even hanging on the sides taken up by fearless travellers. How they collect the fares or maintain any accurate timetable was a source of great speculation and, of course, when the trains have one of their many accidents, owing to the overcrowding, there is awful carnage.

Trying to find the road to Kanpur through a confusing maze of streets took its time but at least it gave us the chance to stop at another railway station for some breakfast. The grand trunk road was impressive but an undeserving title for our route north.

A less crowded train than usual, with for once no passengers on the carriage roofs

Chapter 9

A CONFUSION OF SIGHTS AND SMELLS

Through India to Patna

Standard traffic on the appropriately named 'trunk road'

THERE WAS ONE single track of tarmac necessitating a rapid change of course to dodge any oncoming buses, lorries and in one case a mounted elephant who, quite rightly, took advantage of its intimidating size and momentum – or, in the case of the latter, lack of it! Cyclists were now everywhere and at the next small town we were almost engulfed by a swarm of tuk-tuks which, without question, were trying to intimidate us. We took the majority view of 'we are larger than you' and when for the umpteenth time one deliberately crossed our front it was 'unfortunate' that Gordon's right foot didn't quite make contact with the brake pedal! Land Rover 1, Tuk-Tuk O, with a yellow card, buckled wheel and reproachful look. Forty miles before Kanpur, a large signpost advised us to go straight on for Allahabad, which would by-pass Kanpur and reduce mileage. What started off as an excellent new road soon deteriorated into the more common pothole-dodging dust road. In a way it was lucky progress was slowed, as we were getting low on fuel, and after a further 70 miles we regained some tarmac shortly before reaching Allahabad. Again, the first rest house refused us a room, endorsing our previous experiences of Brits not being welcome. However, we found another one further in the town, where the manager agreed to rent us a room – provided, yet again, we left at dawn. We never did quite work out why it was conditional to vacate by dawn and put it down to the ever-present resentment of the British.

We awoke to be greeted by a very flat tyre, which we knew full well wasn't a coincidence as once I got the wheel off there was no sign of a puncture. I was glad the sun wasn't up whilst I was making the change as it was already very hot. The rest house had proved to be a complete dud ,with hostility, threats and no running water, so after I cleaned myself up we made a Le Mans-type start exit and took much pleasure in seeing the manager emerge irate at our sudden departure to the railway station for breakfast.

Allahabad is one of India's holy cities and is on the confluence of the Yamuna and Ganges rivers. The sacred Ganges is the lifeline to more than 500 million people across India and is worshipped as 'Ganga Mata', the divine mother who sustained life and has nurtured their civilisation for thousands of years. A constant stream of pilgrims visit the city to cast flowers on the river and bathe, from which they derive either spiritual relief or some terminal disease. We had an interesting chat with a garage owner who advised us it took seven years and huge taxes to import a car or if it was a popular make took fourteen! No, we didn't want to sell our Land Rover thank you, and we headed to Patna in the foothills of Northern India. The most popular car in India was the Amby (short for Ambassador), which was based on the British Morris Oxford. It was built from production machines and tools imported from Britain commencing in 1958 and became the most popular car in the country.

We passed a pile of melons nearly up to the first-floor windows of an adjacent house and crossed the swollen Ganges, whose waters had already swamped many of the shanties built on its banks. The 'Grand Trunk' road was not at all grand in our estimation but lived up to its trunk nomenclature, as we saw many elephants with mahout astride carrying or towing logs or firewood. We stopped to introduce ourselves, and Gordon was promptly given a trumpeted shower by the elephant, who was obviously concerned at being photographed.

By the time we reached Varanasi, India's holiest city, it was midday and seriously hot. Varanasi, also known as Benares, is considered the spiritual capital of India and has been the cultural centre of the north for several thousand years. Mark Twain wrote of the city: 'Benares is older than history, older than tradition, older even than legend, and looks twice as old as all of them put together.'

All we could think about were ice cool lagers and an equally cold shower. No chance of either. The crowds, the traffic, the tuk-tuks, the colours and the din of a constant jostling throng, all of whom seemed to have a bell of some sort, surpassed any comparison to date. Whilst asking directions to the Post Office we met a lady who was the matron in charge of the local hospital and after several cups of tea offered to show us

'Matron', our generous guide in Benares

around this teeming city. Delighted to accept, we enjoyed jugs of iced water sitting under overhead fans running at peak revs.

Thus, late that afternoon we sharpened our elbows and forced our way through countless bicycles and headed out to Sarnath. Here was the spot where Buddha 'got the message' and preached his first sermon. In a nearby house is a gold image of him, and his life history is depicted on the walls. From start to finish we were closely watched by the resident manager who, then and only then, advised us there was a charge for every photo taken. A typical example of Indian avariciousness, which has caused so much resentment, particularly in East Africa where they have a monopoly of the small shops known as *dukas* and are renowned for exploiting the luckless African.

Dusk was fast approaching, but we got back to matron's house without damaging any more tuk-tuks or bicycle incidents. Now we were to witness completely different sites which are unknown to the vast majority of tourists. We wove our way through crowds of people and animals to the banks of the river Ganges and we were in a world of paganism, religious fervour, suffering, squalor and death. The smell was awful. The river banks are lined with tiers of terraces, like rows of seats in a football stadium, which are called 'ghats'.

Varanasi, also known as Benares, India's holiest city and principal burial site

At the water's edge were moored many small boats interspersed with religious ceremonies. We took one of these boats and made our way gently downstream, keeping clear of the many people bathing in the dark brown, filthy water. Wherever a Hindu lived and however long it might take, it is their belief that they must end their days at this holy site, which will bring them salvation. The burial processes were taking place all the time. If you were poor you were wrapped in a sheet and weighed down with stones, and one of the boats would take the body out to mid-river where it was tipped overboard. The other final rite was for the more affluent (no pun intended!). In this instance the body is burnt on the riverbank, but there is a fee for the firewood; a priest overseeing the ceremony; ghee (clarified melted butter) to be poured over the body to make it more flammable, a person to break up the skull and bones and then dispose of the subsequent ashes into the river. From our boat in the middle of the river, we witnessed both these processes but kept our distance, not wishing to cause offence. I have to say had we known what we were going to be shown I doubt we would have gone. The banks were literally covered with dead and dying bodies, but one had to remember that it was the choice of each and every one of these people.

Mid-stream in the Ganges, en route to the burial sites

Even so, it was quite unnerving to pick one's way back to the car through all this horrendous suffering. We were happy to leave this behind and, at the exhortations of a white 'holy man' with an enormous long beard and long, lank, ginger hair, we visited a recently constructed Hindu temple. The service was 'conducted' by a man with the biggest stomach I had ever seen with a long pigtail down his back and his only 'clothing' a scanty yellow loincloth. The noises he was uttering were totally indecipherable and were accompanied by much wailing and clanking. A bowl of burning coals was passed around, and each attendant held their hands over it and rubbed their faces. The temple had a multiplicity of shrines, all bedecked with fresh flowers dedicated to an individual god.

The contrast of a delicious Indian dinner and a comfy bed (the last one being in Beirut) at matron's home was very thought-provoking after what we had witnessed that afternoon. Matron urged us to stay on for a while, which was very generous but we were keen to press on. Not least she was keen to show us the pornographic Karma Sutra temple where, gossip had it, Stephen Ward took back some of the techniques for the enjoyment of Christine Keeler! (They had both been key players in the Profumo scandal the year before.) Even as we left Benares we passed a cart and a group, both carrying a body destined for the Ganges – I just pray the river never dries up!

Some 80 miles further on, we turned off our so-called 'Grand' trunk road towards Patna onto a much narrower one with frequent railway crossings. This area was much more widely cultivated, probably with better rainfall and irrigation than the dry, flat plains we had previously covered, owing to the proximity of the Himalaya mountains to the north. The lush green fields were festooned with brightly covered linen and clothing drying in the hot sun. We had a spot of bother with a truck which refused to move over steadfastly ignoring all honking and flashing, but eventually after forcing our way past, we made our frustration apparent which included gestures not in the Highway Code!

Patna, the capital of India's Bihar province and the second largest city after Calcutta/Kolkata in Eastern India, brought its frustrations, as just before reaching the town we crossed one of the tributaries feeding the Ganges to be advised the main bridge we needed was 'just down the river'. After several miles we concluded we had been misinformed so returned to renew our enquiries.

'Indeed, there is a bridge, but it's some 70 miles downriver, or you can take the alternative and cross by ferry, but it has a habit of getting stuck mid-river for indefinite periods.'

We thus concluded that our best cause of action was to carry on downriver, to cross the bridge and return to Patna.

Chapter 10

PEAKS NOT CLOUDS

Journey's end: Nepal

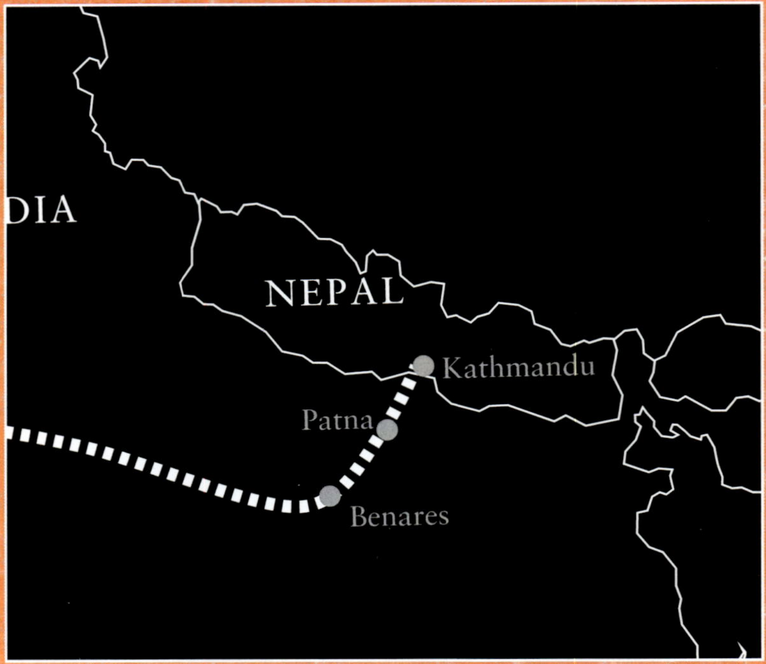

Forever ascending towards the snow-capped Himalayas

WE LEFT PATNA heading due north, and after rounding a bend on the horizon stretching from east to west we were confronted by a line of snow-covered peaks – one of the most unforgettable sights of the journey and a fitting climax. 'No, those are not clouds – they are the Himalayas,' said Gordon. We had taken a halt on the ever-twisting, sinuous route from the plains of India up through the foothills to the Kingdom of Nepal. The distance from Patna to its capital, Kathmandu, was just under 150 miles, but the time element was a totally different matter, obliterating all thoughts of getting to our final destination in the early afternoon. The road was narrow so when you met descending traffic you had to stop and gently squeeze past. From valley floor (100 feet above sea level) to Kathmandu which is just under 5000 feet higher, we progressed slowly but surely. The 120-mile road climb, with one hairpin bend after another, took us nine hours. Maybe a timely reminder of 13,700 miles covered since leaving London!

Kathmandu is the largest centre of population in Nepal's Himalaya Region, with the majority of its inhabitants either Hindu or Buddhist. The Kingdom has a long history of a ruling monarchy and is situated at the crossroads of many ancient Asian civilisations and trading routes.

Foothills of Nepal

Temples, Kathmandu

One of our last major decisions was where to camp in such a concentration of houses and people. Somehow we arrived at the Key Royal Hotel, which was surrounded by gardens and hosted by the jovial Russian proprietor, Boris Lissanevitch, who was more than happy to let us camp on his front lawn. His philosophy was, 'If you have made it this far, you can stay in my grounds and have a bath!' The hotel was converted from a former Rana Palace in the early 1950s by Boris, who had previously been a chef, ballet dancer and a Russian army deserter. It was Nepal's first luxury hotel and catered for many Western dignitaries and tourists. Initially there wasn't any serious competition and it became a famous destination in foreign circles, but as time went by more prestigious hotels were built and it closed five years later. Journey's end.

We stayed in Kathmandu for two weeks, enjoying a mixed climate of cool breezes, occasional showers and sunshine. We visited the sites including the Royal Palace, the zoo – where the American Ambassador's wife's Siamese cat had become an exhibit – and the famous, Pagoda-styled Maru Satta temple built entirely of wood with no metal fittings of any sort. The Nepalese are famed for their cheerful and very brave Gurkha soldiers, one of whom presented me with a Kukri knife. This curved blade can be used in a domestic situation as a machete or as a traditional weapon of the Gurkhas. Its scabbard also houses three smaller knives, two for eating and the other for honing it to a lethal, razor-sharp finish. As it happened, Gordon had brought one from London which he had retrieved from a scrap heap. He was offered five pounds for it. He declined, and a Gurkha major examined it and told him that judging by its blade and shape, it was probably over a hundred years old. Also its ornate handle indicated it was ceremonial and could have been taken from a visiting prime minister who met Queen Victoria in 1850. Because of its cultural and historic significance, it had to be spirited out of the country. The Gurkha regiments have a much larger ceremonial version used reputedly to take off a bull's head in one blow.

We became either 'curiosities' or so-called 'celebrities', depending on your viewpoint. Amongst the stream of visitors we met were the British Ambassador, John Swire, Chairman of Cathay Pacific who gave me his card and told me to get in touch on arrival in Australia. To my eternal regret, I forgot all about this generous invitation and with his help might well have found a more exciting job when I eventually got to Melbourne. Nick Ecker-Ratz of the American Peace Corps was a huge support in assisting Gordon, who was valiantly coping with the demands of our trip but was still far from well. Somewhat disturbingly, to say the least, after a visit to the Mission Hospital, Gordon was examined by an Australian doctor who asked him to step up onto a small stool and advised him he had contracted polio and should see a neurologist on arrival in Melbourne.

I was invited by the Nepalese Minister of Sport to visit his home and view his sporting memorabilia collection, all in glass cases. He was in every team, with his photograph and appropriately crossed table tennis bats, his football boots or a mounted pistol all suitably inscribed with the team details and date. We had a happy but somewhat subdued evening with an American climbing team, some of whom were still coping with the effects of frostbite, who had recently returned from a summit attempt of Everest.

After two weeks of adjusting to a somewhat anti-climatic routine, the realisation and discipline of returning to the 'real' world was proving difficult for both of us. Notwithstanding, the priority was for Gordon to have ongoing medical attention and the opportunity to rest and recuperate until he was strong enough to travel, which meant going our separate ways. Gordon was to be looked after by Bernie Challoner, who was an American Peace Corps doctor, until he considered him fit enough to travel.

Originally we had planned to drive through Assam, Burma (now Myanmar) and through Malaysia down to Singapore, then ship to Perth in Western Australia and drive across the Nullabor Plain to Wagga Wagga in New South Wales. Obviously now, such plans were void, including my brief contemplation of hitchhiking the remainder of our originally proposed route.

We quickly sold all our equipment, including the medical supplies, some packets of soup and my well-worn desert boots for 12 shillings! The sale of our heroic, trusty Land Rover took longer, and Gordon stayed on for a further week to finalise negotiations and payment. All payments were in Nepalese rupees, which would command little in exchange rates, so I invested my share in a plane ticket and flew to Nairobi via Bombay (now Mumbai), as once bitten by the 'African Bug' it never leaves you. I subsequently spent time working on a farm near Lake Naivasha and then hitchhiked through central Africa, crossed Lake Victoria and eventually to Durban from where I took a boat to Melbourne, there to thankfully catch up with a fully recovered Gordon. This ten-day voyage cost me £60, as I qualified for the Australian immigration programme. Gordon in turn flew to Australia from Kolkata via Bangkok and Singapore, having organised a lift from Kathmandu.

My flight to Kenya was scheduled simply to stop at Mumbai to collect further passengers, but on arrival there was a problem with the aircraft, so those originally on board were taken to an overnight stay at the top local hotel, namely the Taj Mahal. The immaculate, turbaned *maître d'* tried not to roll his eyes when confronted with this young man dressed in shorts and hefting a rucksack. I retreated to my sumptuous room and on opening the curtains the following morning was confronted with a scene of total pandemonium. People were running amok all over the streets, wailing, genuflecting, praying and tearing their clothes! It was the 23d May, 1964 and President Jawaharal Nehru had died...

Rare single-horned Asian rhino

I have written this some 60 years after completing this fantastic, memorable journey. Thus it does not reflect so many of the changes, both in name and politically, to the places we travelled. There have been countless atrocities and tragedies since in so many of the countries we visited. Many of the sites we saw have become World Heritage Sites but in spite of this, many have suffered desecration, such as Leptis Magna, Krak des Chevaliers and Palmyra. We were very privileged to visit them. In fact, it would be madness today to attempt a similar route – but we were told that then!

Ten days after leaving school, Robert Grant enlisted in the Scots Guards and progressed to the Royal Military Academy, Sandhurst. A knee injury terminated his military career. After the epic journey described in *Road to Ruins*, he flew to Kenya and hitchhiked through Uganda, Burundi, Rwanda, Zambia, Zimbabwe, South Africa to Durban to sail to Australia. He has motor raced throughout Europe, including Le Mans, and competed in Mexico's Carrera Panamericana, Targa Tasmania and the Springbok Series in Southern Africa.

Robert bought the name of the outerwear brand Puffa a few months after its inception, building it up to Royal Warrant qualification; the word, especially in the form 'puffa jacket', is now essentially a generic term. He now lives in Perthshire.